DINOSAURS

DINOSAURS

Miles
KeLLY

First published in 2009 by Miles Kelly Publishing Ltd
Harding's Barn, Bardfield End Green, Thaxted, Essex, CM6 3PX, UK

Copyright © Miles Kelly Publishing Ltd 2009

This edition printed in 2011

4 6 8 10 9 7 5 3

Publishing Director Belinda Gallagher
Creative Director Jo Cowan
Series and Volume Designer Helen Bracey
Cover Designer Simon Lee
Indexer Gill Lee
Production Manager Elizabeth Collins
Reprographics Anthony Cambray,
Stephan Davis, Ian Paulyn
Assets Lorraine King, Cathy Miles
Contributers Andrew Campbell, Dr Jim Flegg,
Rupert Matthews, Steve Parker

ISBN 978-1-84810-145-6

Printed in China

British Library Cataloguing-in-Publication Data
A catalogue record for this book is available from the British Library

Made with paper from a sustainable forest

www.mileskelly.net
info@mileskelly.net

www.factsforprojects.com

Self-publish your
children's book

buddingpress.co.uk

Contents

Ancient life

Dinosaurs

Age of mammals

Humans

Ancient life

Prehistoric time

Time since the Earth formed is divided into large units called eras, which are in turn divided into periods. Some periods split further into epochs. These units of time relate to the formation of rock layers.

The Precambrian Era ran from 4600–542 million years ago (mya). It saw the beginning of life in the seas. In the Cambrian Period (542–490 mya) the seas were dominated by the first vertebrates.

During the Ordovician Period (490–435 mya) plants began to grow on land. In the Silurian Period (435–410 mya) the first jawed fish appeared, together with the first upright-standing land plants.

The Devonian Period (410–355 mya) witnessed the development of bony fish in the seas, and trees and insects on land.

The Carboniferous Period (355–298 mya) was the time of the great tropical forests and the first land animals with backbones.

During the Permian Period (298–250 mya) reptiles became the dominant land creatures.

The Triassic Period (251–200 mya) saw the rise of the dinosaurs and the first small mammals. In the Jurassic Period (200–145 mya) reptiles dominated the land, sea and sky.

The **Cretaceous Period** (145–65 mya) saw the proliferation of flowering plants, but its end also saw the extinction of the dinosaurs.

The **Tertiary Period** (65–1.6 mya) saw the successful development of mammals and grassland habitats, as well as cooling temperatures.

The **Quaternary Period** (1.6 mya–present) has witnessed the most recent series of ice ages and the rise of modern humans.

▼ *Even though many kinds of animals and plants died out 65 mya, other groups lived on. Insects, worms, fish, birds and mammals all survived the mass extinction and these groups are still alive today.*

Earliest plants

The very first living things on Earth were single-celled bacteria and cyanobacteria, also known as blue-green algae.

Blue-green algae emerged around 3500 mya.

Although it is not a plant, blue-green algae contains chlorophyll and was the first living thing to photosynthesize (make energy from sunlight).

Photosynthesis also produces oxygen. Over millions of years, the blue-green algae produced enough oxygen to enable more complex life forms to develop.

▲ *Lichens such as these are made up of an alga and a fungus. Early lichens – like modern-day ones – grew on rocks and, over time, eroded part of the rock and helped form soil.*

▲ *Lichens can survive in many places where other plants would die, such as the Arctic, on mountaintops and in deserts. Some Arctic lichens are over 4000 years old.*

- **True algae**, which are usually regarded as plants, developed around 1000 mya.

- **By about 550 mya**, multi-celled plants had begun to appear, including simple seaweeds.

- **Algae and lichens** were the first plants to appear on land.

- **Bryophyte plants** (mosses and liverworts) emerged on land around 440 mya. Bryophytes are simple green seedless plants.

- **Unlike vascular plants**, which emerged later, bryophytes cannot grow high above the ground because they do not have strengthened stems.

DID YOU KNOW?

Liverworts grew on mats of blue-green algae, which trapped nitrogen from the air. Liverworts used this nitrogen to grow.

Vascular plants

- **Vascular plants** are more suited to living on drier land than mosses and liverworts.

- **They have branching stems** with tubelike walls that carry water and nutrients.

- **These stems** and walls also mean the plants can stand tall. Vascular plants have spores (reproductive cells, like seeds) – the taller the plant the more widely it can disperse its spores.

- **One of the first known** vascular plants was *Cooksonia*. It was about 5 cm tall, with a forked stem.

- **Scientists** called palaeontologists discovered fossil remains of *Cooksonia* in Wales. Palaeontologists study fossils of prehistoric plants and animals to see how they lived and evolved.

- **Rhynie in Scotland** is one site where lots of vascular plant fossils have been found.

- **The plants** at Rhynie would have grown on the sandy edges of pools in the Early Devonian Period (about 400 mya).

- **One plant fossil** found at Rhynie is *Aglaophyton*, which stood around 45 cm high.

- *Aglaophyton* had underground roots and tissues that supported the plant stem. It also had water-carrying tubes and stomata (tiny openings) that allowed air and water to pass through.

- **Land-living plants** were essential for providing conditions for animals to make the transition from the seas to land. They created soil, food and ground cover for shelter.

▲ The Cooksonia *plant had forked stems ending in spore-filled caps. The earliest examples of* Cooksonia *have been found in Ireland, dating to around 430 mya.*

Gymnosperms

- **Gymnosperms** are plants that produce exposed seeds on the surface of structures such as cones. The word gymnosperm comes from two Greek words: *gymnos*, meaning 'naked', and *sperma*, meaning 'seed'.

- **These plants first appeared** about 370 mya. They probably developed from early plants such as *Cooksonia*.

- **Gymnosperms** grew well in the damp, tropical forests of the Carboniferous Period (355–298 mya).

▲ Cycads have fernlike leaves growing in a circle around the end of the stem. New leaves sprout each year and last for several years.

- **Varieties** of gymnosperm include conifers, cycads and seed-ferns.

- **Cycads** are palmlike plants with feathery tops. They were much more common in prehistoric times than they are today.

▶ Also known as maidenhair trees, gingkos are an ancient type of plant with fan-shaped leaves and fleshy yellow seeds.

One type of cycad is the maidenhair tree, *Gingko biloba*. It still grows in towns and cities, but is now very rare in the wild.

One extinct gymnosperm is *Glossopteris*, which some palaeontologists believe is the ancestor of later flowering plants.

Together with ferns and horsetails (a type of herb), gymnosperms dominated landscapes during the Mesozoic Era (251–65 mya).

In the Jurassic Period (200–145 mya), plant-eating dinosaurs ate their way through huge areas of coniferous forest.

Today, conifers are found most often in cold or dry areas, to which they are well adapted.

▲ *Conifer trees have needle-like leaves that make their seeds in cones rather than in flowers.*

▶ *This* Araucaria, *or monkey puzzle tree, is a type of conifer that dates back to the Jurassic Period.*

Angiosperms

Angiosperms are flowering plants. They produce seeds within an ovary, which is contained within a flower. The word comes from the Greek terms *angeion*, meaning 'vessel', and *sperma*, meaning 'seed'.

These plants first appeared about 140 mya.

The earliest evidence of flowering plants comes from the fossil remains of leaves and pollen grains.

Plant experts used to think that magnolias were one of the first angiosperms, but they now think that an extinct plant called *Archaefructus* was older. It lived about 145 mya.

Fossil remains of *Archaefructus* were discovered in northeast China in the mid to late 1990s.

By 100 mya, angiosperms had developed into many dozens of families of flowering plants, most of which still survive today.

By 60 mya, angiosperms had taken over from gymnosperms as the dominant plants on Earth.

The start of the Tertiary Period (around 65 mya) saw a rise in temperatures that produced the right conditions for tropical rainforests.

It was in the rainforests that angiosperms evolved into many different types of plants.

Angiosperms were successful because they could grow very quickly, they had very extensive root systems to anchor them and take up water and nutrients, and they could grow in a greater range of environments than other plants, such as gymnosperms.

▲ An Archaefructus *plant, which some scientists think is the earliest known example of an angiosperm. The* Archaefructus *fossil, which may be around 145 million years old, has a number of angiosperm features including enclosed seeds and flowers.*

The first invertebrates

🐾 **An invertebrate** is an animal that does not have a spinal column. Invertebrates were the first animals to live on Earth, in the prehistoric seas.

🐾 **The very first animal-like** organisms that fed on other organisms or organic matter were single-celled and sometimes called protozoans.

🐾 **Only prehistoric protozoans** with hard parts survive as fossils. The earliest fossils are around 700 million years old.

🐾 **One of the earliest known fossils** of a multi-celled animal is around 600 million years old. This is a creature called *Mawsonites*, which may have been a primitive jellyfish or worm.

🐾 **Most of the earliest** invertebrate fossils are from extinct groups of animals.

🐾 **Some of these animals** had segmented bodies that looked a bit like quilts.

🐾 **One such invertebrate** is *Spriggina*, which is named after Reg Sprigg, a geologist. He discovered its fossilized remains near Ediacara in southern Australia in 1946.

🐾 **Palaeontologists** have unearthed the fossils of many other invertebrates that resemble jellyfish from Ediacara.

DID YOU KNOW?

Spriggina has a curved, shieldlike end to one part of its body. Some palaeontologists think this was its head, while others think it was an anchor that secured it to the seabed.

Another famous invertebrate discovery was made by Roger Mason, an English schoolboy, in 1957. This was the fossil of *Charnia*, an animal that was similar to a living sea pen.

▼ Charnia *was a prehistoric animal that grew in feather-like colonies attached to the seabed, like living sea pens.* Charnia *fossils date to around 700 mya.*

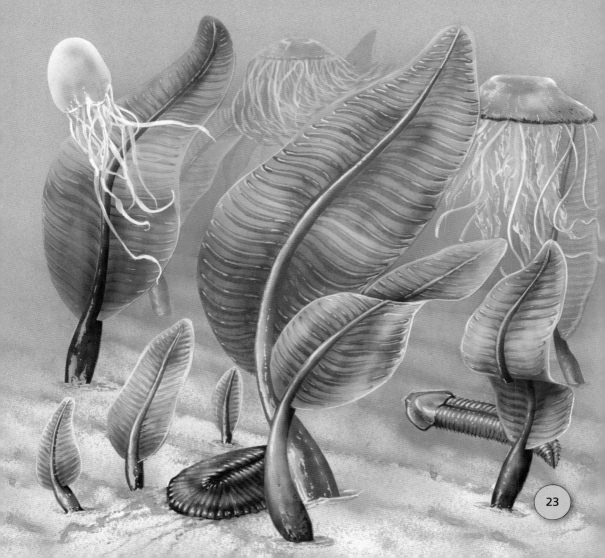

Arthropods

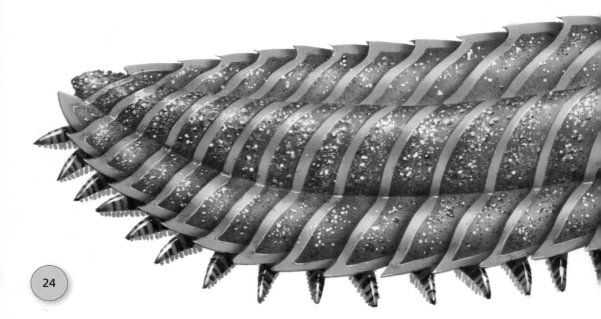

- **Arthropods form** the largest single group of animals. They include insects, crustaceans (crabs or lobsters), arachnids (spiders) and myriapods (millipedes) – any creature with a segmented body and jointed limbs.

- **The earliest known remains** of arthropods come from the 530-million-year-old mudstone deposits of the Burgess Shale in Canada.

- *Marrella* is one of the most common fossils discovered at the Burgess Shale. It was about 2 cm long and had a head shield and two antennae.

- **Its body was divided** into segments, each of which had a jointed leg for scurrying over the seabed.

- **At first**, palaeontologists thought *Marrella* was a trilobite, but they now regard it as an entirely different type of arthropod.

- **One of the first** – if not the first – groups of animals to emerge from the sea and colonize the land were arthropods, some time between 500 and 400 mya.

- **Arthropods** were well suited for living on land. Many of them had exoskeletons (outer skeletons) that prevented them from drying out. Their jointed limbs meant they could move over the ground.

- **Woodlice** may have been the very first arthropods on land. They feed on rotting plant material, which they would have found on seashores.

- **The largest-ever land arthropod** was a millipede-like creature called *Arthropleura* that was 1.8 m long.

- ***Arthropleura* lived on forest floors** during the Carboniferous Period (355–298 mya). Like woodlice, it ate rotting plants.

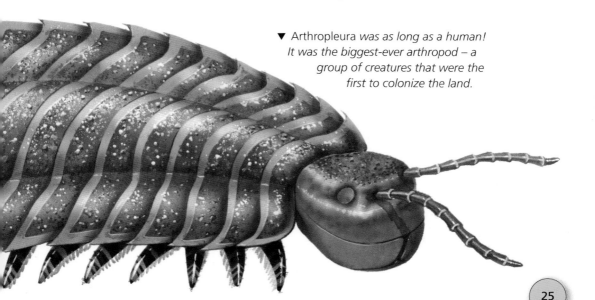

▼ Arthropleura *was as long as a human! It was the biggest-ever arthropod – a group of creatures that were the first to colonize the land.*

Molluscs and graptolites

- **Modern molluscs** include gastropods (slugs, snails and limpets), bivalves (clams, oysters, mussels and cockles) and cephalopods (octopuses, squids and cuttlefish).

- **Modern and prehistoric molluscs** represent one of the most diverse animal groups ever to have lived.

- **The first molluscs** were tiny – about the size of a pinhead. They appeared at the beginning of the Cambrian Period, about 542 mya.

- **The first cephalopod molluscs** emerged towards the end of the Cambrian Period, around 490 mya.

- **One early cephalopod** was *Plectronoceras*, which had a horn-shaped shell divided into different chambers.

- **Graptolites** had tentacles that they used to sieve food particles from water or the seabed.

- **Gastropod molluscs** (snails and slugs) were one of the first groups of animals to live on land.

- **Snails and slugs** are limited to where they can live on land as they require moist conditions.

- **Cephalopods** are the most highly developed of all molluscs. Squids and octopuses evolved big brains, good eyesight, tentacles and beaklike jaws.

Graptolites are an extinct group of molluscs that lived in string-like communities. Graptolite means 'written stone' because the fossils of these creatures resemble scrawled handwriting.

◄ *This snail is a mollusc. Its features include a muscular foot, a head with eyes and tentacles, and a shell. Today there are more than 100,000 living species of molluscs but many more lived in the past. They are very important as their shells make good fossils and some types evolve quickly, so their rapid-changing shapes are used as 'marker fossils' to date rocks.*

Ammonites

- **Ammonites** belong to the cephalopod group of molluscs. They were once widespread in the oceans, but, like the dinosaurs, died out at the end of the Cretaceous Period (about 65 mya).

- **The number** of ammonite fossils that have been found proves how plentiful these animals once were.

- **Ammonites** were predators and scavengers. They had very good vision, long seizing tentacles and powerful mouths.

- **Their mouths** consisted of sharp beaks, poisonous glands and a tooth-covered tongue.

- **Ammonites** had multi-chambered shells that contained gas and worked like flotation tanks, keeping the creatures afloat.

- *Stephanoceras* was an ammonite with a spiral, disc-shaped shell, 20 cm across. It was very common in the seas of the Mesozoic Era.

- **The closest living** relative of ammonites is *Nautilus*, a cephalopod that lives near the seabed and feeds on shrimps.

Chambers

▶ A rock containing an ammonite fossil, clearly displaying the shell's division into different chambers. The innermost chamber was the home of a newborn ammonite. As it grew, it built a bigger chamber and moved into it. When it outgrew that chamber it built another one, and so on, to form a spiral-patterned shell.

People once thought that ammonite fossils were the fossils of curled-up snakes.

Builders have traditionally set ammonite fossils into the walls of buildings for decoration.

▼ *An ammonite swims through the sea in search of food.*
The animal swam backwards, with its tentacles trailing behind.

Trilobites

- **Trilobites** belonged to the invertebrate group called arthropods – animals with segmented bodies and hard outer skeletons.

- **The name trilobite** means 'three lobes'. Trilobites' hard outer shells were divided into three parts.

- **The first trilobites** appeared about 530 mya. By 500 mya, they had developed into many different types.

- **These invertebrates** had compound eyes, like insects' eyes, which could see in many different directions at once.

- **Some trilobites** could roll up into a ball, like some woodlice do today. This was a useful means of protection.

- **Long, thin, jointed legs** enabled trilobites to move quickly over the seabed or sediment covering it.

- **Trilobites** moulted by shedding their outer skeletons. Most trilobite fossils are the remains of these shed skeletons.

- **One of the largest known trilobites** was *Isotelus*, which grew up to 44 cm long.

- **Other trilobites were** much smaller, such as *Conocoryphe*, which was about 2 cm long.

- **Trilobites** became extinct around 250 mya – along with huge numbers of other marine animals.

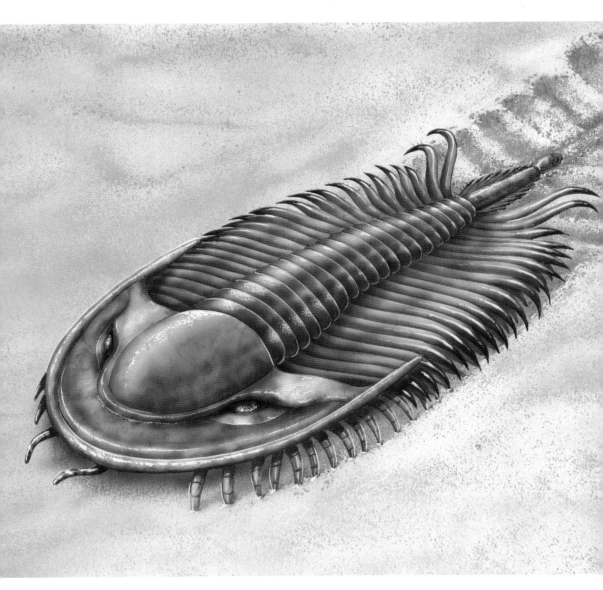

▲ *This* Conocoryphe *trilobite lived in the seas of the Mid Cambrian Period, about 530 mya. It was one of the smaller trilobites.*

Pikaia

- **A small, wormlike creature** called *Pikaia* is thought to be the ancestor of all backboned animals.

- **Its fossil remains** were found in the 530-million-year-old mudstone deposits of the Burgess Shale in Canada.

- *Pikaia* was the first known chordate, a group of animals with a stiff supporting rod, called a notochord, along their back. All vertebrates belong to this group, as well as marine animals called tunicates and acraniates.

- *Pikaia* **was 5 cm long** with a notochord (stiffening rod) running along its body – a kind of primitive spine that gave its body flexibility.

- **The notochord** also allowed the animal's simple muscles to work against it, and the animal's body organs to hang from it.

- *Pikaia* is very similar to a modern creature called *Branchiostoma*, a small, transparent creature that lives in the sand at the bottom of the sea.

- **As it lacks** a bony skeleton, paired fins and jaws, *Pikaia* is not really a fish.

- *Pikaia* is a more complex creature than many other animals found in the Burgess Shale. It suggests that other complex creatures must have lived before it, although there is (as yet) no fossil evidence for this.

The head of the *Pikaia* was very primitive with a pair of tentacles, a mouth and a simple brain (a swelling of the nerve cord) for processing information.

Pikaia swam in a zig-zag fashion, similar to a sea snake.

▼ Pikaia *looked a little like an eel with tail fins. The stiff rod that ran along its body developed into the backbone in later animals.*

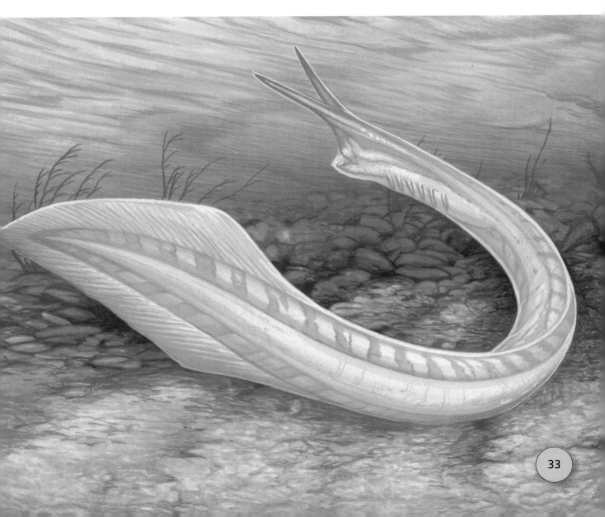

Jawless fish

The first fish appeared in the Late Cambrian Period about 500 mya.

These fish had permanently gaping mouths – as they had no jaws they could not open and close their mouths.

▼ *Early jawless fish such as* Hemicyclaspis *could swim much farther and quicker than most invertebrates. This meant they could more easily search for and move to new feeding areas.*

- **Early fish** were called agnathans, which means 'jawless'.

- **Agnathans** ate by sieving plankton through their simple mouth opening, as well as scooping up algae on the seabed.

- **Among the oldest** complete agnathan fossils are *Arandaspis*, which comes from Australia, and *Sacabambaspis*, which comes from Bolivia.

- *Hemicyclaspis* was another agnathan. It was a flat fish with a broad head shield and a long tail.

- **Later jawless fish** had more streamlined, rounder bodies and eyes at the front of their heads. This suggests they were not restricted to the seabed.

- **Most jawless fish** died out by the end of the Devonian Period (around 350 mya).

- **Living relatives of agnathans** include lampreys and hagfish, which have soft bodies and look like eels. Like agnathans, they are also jawless.

DID YOU KNOW?
Hemicyclaspis had eyes on top of its head. This suggests it lived on the seabed and used its eyes to keep a lookout for predators above.

Jawed fish

- **The first jawed fish** emerged in the Early Silurian Period (about 430 mya).

- **Palaeontologists** call jawed fish acanthodians, a name that comes from the Greek word *akantha*, meaning 'thorn' or 'spine'.

- **Jaws and teeth** gave acanthodians a huge advantage over jawless fish – they could eat a greater variety of food and defend themselves more effectively.

- **Jaws and teeth** allowed acanthodians to become predators.

- **Acanthodians' jaws** evolved from structures called gill arches in the pharynx, the tube in vertebrates that runs from the mouth to the stomach.

- **Gill arches** are bony rods and muscles that surround the gills, the breathing organs of a fish.

- **As acanthodians** developed jaws, so they developed teeth, too.

- **The earliest** fish teeth were conelike shapes along the jaw, made out of bone and coated with hard enamel.

- **The teeth** of early acanthodians varied greatly. In some species they were sharp and spiky, in others they were like blades, while in others they resembled flat plates.

DID YOU KNOW?
Another difference between jawed and jawless fish was that jawed fish had a pair of nostrils, while jawless fish only had one.

▲ Climatius, *a type of acanthodian or jawed fish, lived around 400 mya. Another name for acanthodians is 'spiny sharks' – although they were not sharks, many had spines on the edges of their fins.*

Sharks

The earliest known shark fossils come from rock layers of the Early Devonian Period (410–355 mya).

Sharks belong to the group known as cartilaginous fish, which also includes rays and skates. Their skeletons are made from cartilage, not bone.

Cladoselache was a prehistoric shark, which could grow up to 2 m long.

Cladoselache appears to have been quite similar to a modern shark – it had a streamlined body, a pair of dorsal (back) fins and triangular-shaped pectoral (front end) fins.

Early sharks hunted squid, small fish and crustaceans.

Stethacanthus was a prehistoric shark that looked nothing like a modern one. It had an anvil-shaped projection above its head, which was covered in teeth.

DID YOU KNOW?

Prehistoric sharks' jaws were fixed to the side of their skull, while modern sharks' jaws hang beneath their braincase, which gives them a more powerful bite.

▼ This modern blue shark is a fast swimmer and a fierce hunter. The main features of sharks – from their tightly packed, needle-sharp teeth to their streamlined shape – have changed little over 400 million years.

38

● **Stethacanthus** lived in the Carboniferous Period (355–298 mya).

● **Sharks are at the top** of the food chain in modern seas, but this was not the case during the Devonian Period.

● **Other Devonian fish** were much larger than the prehistoric sharks. For example, *Dunkleosteus* grew to be up to 3.7 m long and would have been able to snap up any contemporary shark in a flash.

▼ Hybodus *was a blunt-headed prehistoric shark that lived between 250 and 125 mya in the time of the dinosaurs. It looked quite similar to modern sharks, but had very different jaws.*

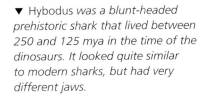

Bony fish

- **Bony fish** have internal skeletons and external scales made of bone.

- **They first appeared** in the Late Devonian Period (around 360 mya).

- **Bony fish** evolved into the most abundant and varied fish in the seas.

- **There are two types** of bony fish – ray-finned fish and lobe-finned fish.

- **There were plenty** of prehistoric lobe-finned fish, but only a few species survive today. They belong to one of two groups – lungfish or coelacanths.

- **Amphibians** – and ultimately reptiles and mammals – evolved from lobe-finned fish.

- **Ray-finned fish** were so-called because of the bony rays that supported their fins. Most early ray-finned fish were small, ranging in size from about 5–20 cm long.

- *Rhadinichthys* **and** *Cheirolepis* were two early ray-finned fish. They were small predators equipped with good swimming ability and snapping jaws.

- **Around 250 mya**, ray-finned fish lost many of the bony rays from their fins. The fins became more flexible and the fish became better swimmers.

- **New types of ray-finned fish**, called teleosts, also developed more symmetrical tails and thinner scales.

▼ This modern-day coelacanth is a direct descendant of the lobe-finned bony fish that lived 350 mya. Coelacanths were thought to be extinct until a fisherman caught one off the coast of South Africa in 1938.

From fins to limbs

- **The first land-dwelling**, backboned animals were called tetrapods. They needed legs to hold up their bodies and move around in search of water and food.

- **Tetrapods** evolved from lobe-finned fish, which had all the right body parts to develop arms and legs.

- **The fossil skeleton** of the lobe-finned fish *Eusthenopteron* shows that the organization of bones in its front and rear fins was similar to the arrangement of limbs in tetrapods.

- *Eusthenopteron* lived in shallow waters. It could use its fins as primitive legs and move over land if the waters dried out.

- **Recent research suggests** that another lobe-finned fish, *Panderichthys*, could use its fins more effectively as limbs than *Eusthenopteron*. According to scientists, *Panderichthys* was more like a tetrapod than a fish.

- **The front fins** in lobe-finned fish connected to a shoulder girdle, while the rear fins connected to a hip girdle. These girdles connected to the backbone.

- **These hip and shoulder** connections meant that the limbs of future tetrapods were connected to a skeleton, which prevented the limbs from pressing against the inside of the body and damaging it.

The shoulder girdle of lobe-finned fish also connected to their heads. Tetrapods, however, developed heads that were separated from their shoulders and joined instead by a neck.

Necks were a great advantage to land-living animals. They could use them to bend down, to reach up, and to turn around to see in other directions.

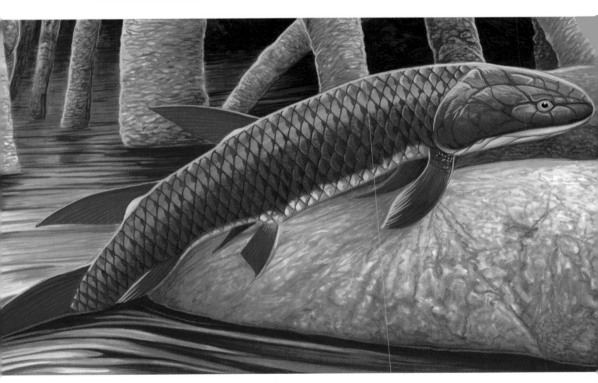

▲ Eusthenopteron *using its fins to move out of the water. Eusthenopteron, which means 'good strong fin', was once thought to be the closest ancestor to tetrapods. However palaeontologists have recently discovered that another fish,* Panderichthys, *was an even closer relative.*

43

Breathing air

- **Fish breathe oxygen** in water through their gills. When a fish is out of the water, these gills collapse.

- **For creatures to adapt** to living on land, they had to develop air-breathing lungs.

- **Tetrapods** were not the first creatures to develop lungs – this step was taken by lobe-finned fish.

- **Lungfish** are lobe-fins that still exist today. They live in hot places and when rivers dry out, they bury themselves in mud and breathe through lungs.

- **Early tetrapods**, such as *Ichthyostega* and *Acanthostega*, had gills and lungs, which suggests they could breathe both air and water.

- **Later tetrapods** breathed through gills when they were first born, but, like modern frogs and newts, their gills became smaller as they got older and were replaced by lungs.

- **Modern amphibians** also take in oxygen through their skin, which is soft and moist.

- **Early tetrapods** had tougher skin, so were unable to breathe through it.

- **Breathing through skin** limits an animal's size, which is why modern amphibians are much smaller than many of their prehistoric ancestors.

DID YOU KNOW?
Animals could only evolve to live on land because of the work of plants over millions of years, producing oxygen that became part of Earth's atmosphere.

▼ Prehistoric lungfish had lungs as well as gills.
Like these modern lungfish, they were
able to breathe air if the pools or
rivers they lived in dried out.

45

Acanthostega

▲ Acanthostega *may have evolved from lobe-finned fish such as* Eusthenopteron *and* Panderichthys. *It shared a number of features with these fish, including a similar set of gills and lungs, as well as a tail fin and braincase.*

- *Acanthostega* was one of the earliest tetrapods. It had a fishlike body, which suggests it spent most of its life in water.

- **Fossil remains** of *Acanthostega* were found in rock strata dating from the Late Devonian Period (around 370 mya).

DID YOU KNOW?
Acanthostega had fishlike gills for breathing water as well as lungs for breathing air.

- *Acanthostega's* **body** was about one metre long.

- **These tetrapods had** wide tails that would have been useful for swimming but inconvenient for moving on land.

- *Acanthostega's* **legs**, however, were well-developed, with eight toes on the front feet and seven on the rear ones.

- **The number of toes** on its feet surprised palaeontologists – they had previously thought all tetrapods had five toes.

- *Acanthostega's* **legs and toes** would have helped to give its body a thrusting motion when it swam. They would also aid movement through plants at the bottom of rivers and lakes in search of prey.

- *Acanthostega* had a flattened skull and its eye sockets were placed close together on the top of its head.

- **A complete** but jumbled-up *Acanthostega* fossil was discovered in hard rock in Greenland. Palaeontologists had to work very carefully to prise the fossil from the rock.

Frogs and salamanders

🦶 **Modern amphibians**, such as frogs, toads, salamanders and newts, all belong to the group called the lissamphibians.

🦶 **Lissamphibians** evolved later than the early tetrapods, between the Late Carboniferous and Middle Triassic Periods (300–240 mya).

🦶 *Triadobatrachus* lived in the Early Triassic Period in Madagascar, was 10 cm long and had a froglike skull.

🦶 **Compared to earlier amphibians**, *Triadobatrachus* had a shortened back with fewer spinal bones and a shortened tail.

🦶 **Evolution** did not stop with *Triadobatrachus* – modern frogs have even fewer spinal bones and no tail at all.

🦶 *Triadobatrachus'* hind legs were roughly the same size as its front legs. Again, this is different to modern frogs, which have long hind legs for hopping.

🦶 *Taraurus* is the first known salamander. It lived in the Late Jurassic Period (around 150 mya) in Kazakhstan. It was 19 cm long with a broad skull.

DID YOU KNOW?

Andrias scheuchzerii was a salamander from the Miocene Epoch (23–5 mya). It was named after the Swiss scientist Johannes Scheuchzer, who discovered it in 1726.

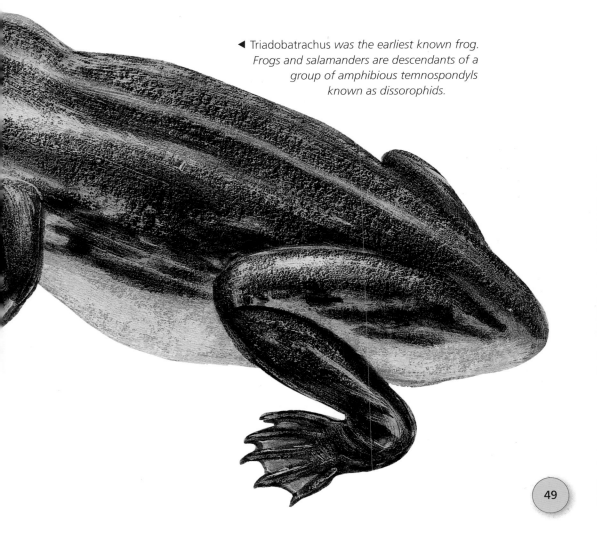

● **More modern-looking frog** and salamander fossils have been discovered in Messel, Germany. They date from the Early Eocene Epoch (around 50 mya).

● **Some Messel frog fossils** have their legs bent as if they were in mid-hop. There are even tadpole fossils from Messel.

◄ Triadobatrachus *was the earliest known frog. Frogs and salamanders are descendants of a group of amphibious temnospondyls known as dissorophids.*

First reptiles

Reptiles evolved from amphibians during the Carboniferous Period (355–298 mya).

Unlike amphibians, which usually live near and lay their eggs in water, reptiles are much more adapted for living on land.

▲ Hylonomus, *meaning 'forest mouse', was one of the earliest reptiles. Fossil hunters discovered its remains in fossilized tree stumps at Joggins in Nova Scotia, Canada.*

- **Compared to amphibians**, reptiles had better limbs for walking, a more effective circulatory system for moving blood around their bodies, and bigger brains.

- **They also had more powerful** jaw muscles than amphibians and would have been better predators. Early reptiles ate millipedes, spiders and insects.

- **One of the earliest reptiles** was a small creature called *Hylonomus*, which lived in the Mid-Carboniferous Period.

- *Hylonomus* lived in forests on the edges of lakes and rivers. Fossil remains of this reptile have been found inside the stumps of clubmoss trees.

- **Another early reptile** was *Paleothyris*. Like *Hylonomus*, it was about 20 cm long and had a smaller head than amphibians.

- **One animal** that represents a staging post between amphibians and reptiles is *Westlothiana lizziae*, which was discovered in Scotland in the 1980s.

- *Westlothiana lizziae* lived in the Early Carboniferous Period (about 340 mya).

- **At first**, palaeontologists thought that *Westlothiana lizziae* was the oldest reptile. However, its backbone, head and legs are closer to those of an amphibian.

Eggs

- **Reptile eggs** are a major evolutionary advance over amphibian eggs.

- **Early amphibians**, like modern ones, laid their eggs in water. This is because their eggs were covered in jelly (like modern frogspawn) and would dry out on land.

- **Reptiles evolved** eggs that were covered by a protective shell. This meant they could lay them on land and they would not dry out.

▲ Frogs lay their eggs in water in jelly-like clumps called spawn.

▲ A female snake protecting her eggs. Eggs laid on land are easier to protect than those laid in water.

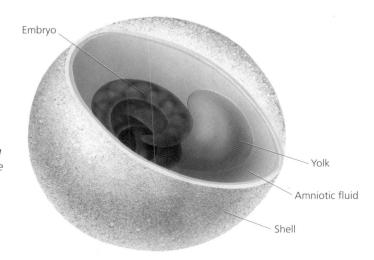

Embryo

Yolk

Amniotic fluid

Shell

▶ *Reptiles broke the link between reproduction and water by laying hard-shelled eggs on land. This snake shell contains the developing young (embryo), a food store (yolk) and a protective liquid (amniotic fluid).*

One advantage of shelled eggs was that reptiles did not have to return to water to lay them.

Another advantage was that reptiles could hide their eggs on land. Eggs laid in water are easy pickings for hungry animals.

Reptile embryos complete all their growth phases inside eggs. When they hatch they look like miniature adults.

In contrast, baby amphibians hatch out of their eggs as larvae, such as tadpoles. They live in water and breathe through gills before they develop lungs and can live on land.

Reptile shells are hard and protect the growing embryos. The eggs also provide the embryos with food while they develop.

During the evolution from amphibians to reptiles, some tetrapods laid jelly-covered eggs on land.

A number of today's amphibians lay jelly-covered eggs on land, including some tropical frogs and mountain salamanders.

Skulls

 The jaws of reptiles are another feature that shows the evolutionary progression from amphibians.

 Amphibian jaws are designed to snap but not to bite together tightly.

 In contrast, reptiles had more jaw muscles and could press their jaws together more firmly. This meant they could break insect body casings and chew through tough plant stems.

 By the Late Carboniferous Period (about 300 mya), reptiles developed openings in their skulls behind the eye socket. These openings allowed room for more jaw muscles.

 Four types of reptile skull developed. Each belonged to a different type of reptile.

 Anapsids had no openings in their skull other than the eye sockets. Turtles and tortoises are anapsids.

 Euryapsids had one opening high up on either side of the skull. Sea reptiles such as ichthyosaurs were euryapsids, but this group has no surviving relatives.

- **Synapsids** had one opening low down on either side of the skull. Mammals are descended from this group.

- **Diapsids** had two openings on either side of the skull. Dinosaurs and pterosaurs were diapsids; so too are birds and crocodiles.

DID YOU KNOW?

Plants developed tough stems and leaves, spines and poisons to protect themselves from hungry reptiles.

▼ Varanosaurus *was a synapsid reptile that lived in North America in the Early Permian Period, about 290 mya. There are important similarities between the skulls of synapsid reptiles and mammals.*

Synapsids

- **Synapsids** were a group of reptiles that had a pair of openings on their lower skull behind the eye socket, onto which their jaw muscles attached.

- **These reptiles** first appeared in the Late Carboniferous Period (about 310 mya). They became the dominant land animals in the Permian and Triassic Periods (299–200 mya).

- **Synapsids are the ancestors** of mammals, which explains why they are sometimes described as 'mammal-like reptiles'.

- **The first synapsids** are called pelycosaurs. They were large, heavy-bodied animals that walked a bit like modern-day crocodiles.

- **The fierce meat eater** *Dimetrodon* and the plant-eating *Edaphosaurus* – both of which had long, fanlike spines on their backs – were pelycosaurs.

- **Later synapsids** are called therapsids. The earliest therapsids had bigger skulls and jaws than pelycosaurs, as well as longer legs and shorter tails.

- **Later therapsids** are divided into two subgroups – dicynodonts and cynodonts. Dicynodont means 'two dog teeth' – cynodont means 'dog tooth'.

- **Dicynodonts** were herbivores. Most had round, hippopotamus-shaped bodies, and beaks that they used to cut plant stems.

Cynodonts were carnivores. They used different teeth in their mouth for different tasks – for stabbing, nipping and chewing.

Of all reptiles, Cynodonts were the most mammal-like. Some had whiskers and may even have been warm-blooded.

▼ Diictodon *was a mammal-like reptile that lived about 260 mya. A plant eater and a burrower,* Diictodon *was an advanced form of a synapsid known as a dicynodont.*

57

Crocodilians

🦶 **The first crocodile-like reptiles** were called eosuchians, meaning 'dawn crocodiles'. They appeared in the Permian Period (298–250 mya).

🦶 **The first true crocodiles** appeared during the Late Triassic Period (about 215 mya). They were called protosuchians and lived in pools and rivers.

🦶 **As its name suggests**, *Protosuchus* was a protosuchian. It had a short skull and sharp teeth, and would have looked quite like a modern crocodile.

🦶 **Other early crocodiles**, such as *Terrestrisuchus*, looked less like modern crocodiles.

🦶 *Terrestrisuchus* had a short body and long legs. Its name means 'land crocodile' because palaeontologists think it may have been more at home on land than in water.

🦶 **The next group** of crocodilians to evolve were the mesosuchians, which lived in the sea.

🦶 *Metriorhynchus* was a marine mesosuchian. It had flippers instead of limbs and very sharp, fish-stabbing teeth. It lived in the Late Jurassic Period (around 150 mya).

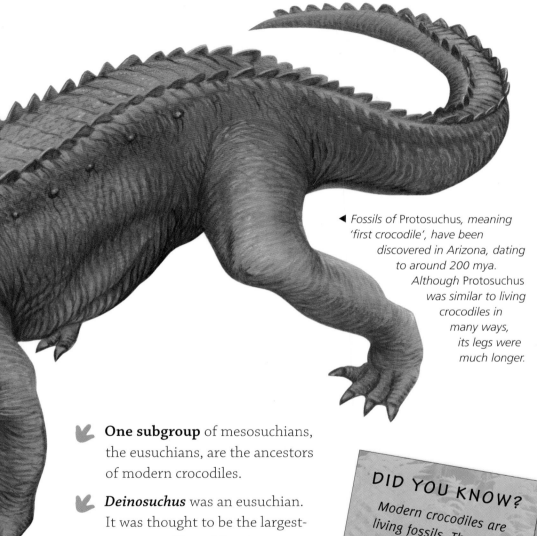

◀ Fossils of Protosuchus, *meaning 'first crocodile', have been discovered in Arizona, dating to around 200 mya. Although Protosuchus was similar to living crocodiles in many ways, its legs were much longer.*

One subgroup of mesosuchians, the eusuchians, are the ancestors of modern crocodiles.

Deinosuchus was an eusuchian. It was thought to be the largest-ever crocodile at 11 m long until a recent discovery of a *Sarchosuchus* fossil, which is estimated to measure 15 m.

DID YOU KNOW?

Modern crocodiles are living fossils. They look similar to the crocodiles that were alive 100 mya.

59

Turtles and tortoises

▲ Proganochelys, *an ancestor of modern turtles and tortoises, had a 60-cm-long shell, but it was unable to pull its head or legs inside.*

Turtles and tortoises both have shells that cover and protect their bodies. They belong to a group of reptiles called chelonians.

Chelonian shells evolved from belly ribs that grew outside of the body.

The earliest chelonian fossils come from the Triassic Period (251–200 mya). They have been found in Germany and Thailand.

One very early chelonian was *Proganochelys*.

Proganochelys had a well-developed, heavily-armoured shell, but palaeontologists think that it could not pull its head, legs or tail inside it.

The ability to pull the head, legs and tail inside the shell is important for turtles and tortoises because it provides them with maximum protection.

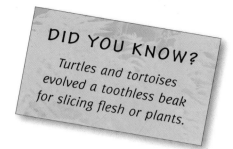

The protective shells of turtles and tortoises may have helped them survive at the end of the Cretaceous Period, 65 mya, when so many other reptiles became extinct.

Tortoises have bigger shells than turtles. This is because they are very slow-moving land creatures – unlike the swimming turtles – and need more protection.

A huge number and variety of turtle fossils have been discovered at Riversleigh in Australia, dating from the Miocene Epoch (23–5 mya).

▶ Archelon *fossils show that it was similar to, but much bigger than, modern leatherback turtles. Its front limbs were thinner and longer than its hind ones and were more useful in the water.*

Snakes

- **The first known snake** is *Dinilysia*, which was found in Argentina and lived in the Late Cretaceous Period, about 80 mya.

- **There are earlier** snakelike fossils, but palaeontologists generally think these were reptiles and not snakes.

- **The ancestors** of snakes were lizards. Palaeontologists think it would have been a varanid lizard, of which the modern monitor lizard is an example.

- **Snakes** are an evolutionary triumph. They are one of the few land-living animals to survive and flourish without limbs.

- **Compared to other reptiles**, snake fossils are rare. This is because snake bones are delicate and do not fossilize well.

- **Snakes evolved** into a huge variety of types in the Tertiary Period (65–1.6 mya). Today, there are more than 2000 snake species living in nearly every type of habitat.

- **The 50 million-year-old fossils** from Messel, Germany, include the well-preserved remains of *Palaeopython*, a 2-m-long early python.

> **DID YOU KNOW?**
> Snakes are one of the few groups of reptiles that had their main evolutionary development after the time of the dinosaurs.

- **Early snakes** killed their prey by squeezing it to death. Modern boas and pythons also use this method to kill.

- **Poisonous snakes,** such as vipers, adders and cobras, did not evolve until the Miocene Epoch (23–5 mya).

▲ *Some scientists argue that modern snakes, like this carpet python, are related to the prehistoric sea reptiles, mosasaurs. Like snakes, mosasaurs' limbs were reduced in size and their bodies were long and flexible.*

Placodonts

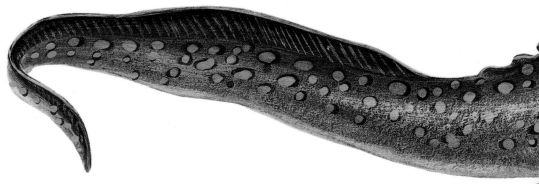

🐾 **After adapting** so well to life on land, some groups of reptiles evolved into water-dwelling creatures.

🐾 **Placodonts** were early aquatic (water-living) reptiles. They lived in the Mid Triassic Period (about 245–228 mya).

🐾 **The name placodont** means 'plate tooth'. These reptiles had large cheek teeth that worked like crushing plates.

🐾 **Placodonts** appeared at about the same time as another group of aquatic reptiles called nothosaurs.

🐾 **They had shorter**, sturdier bodies than the nothosaurs but, like them, they did not survive as a group for long.

🐾 *Placodus* was a placodont. It had a stocky body, stumpy limbs and webbed toes for paddling. It may have had a fin on its tail.

▶ Placodus *grew up to 2 m long and probably used its sticking-out front teeth to scrape up molluscs from the seabed. Its platelike side teeth would then make short work of crunching the molluscs.*

- *Placodus* means 'flat tooth'. It probably used its flat teeth, which pointed outwards from its mouth, to prise shellfish off rocks.

- *Psephoderma* was a turtle-like placodont. Its body was covered in a shell, which was covered by hard plates.

- *Psephoderma* also had a horny beak, like a turtle's, and paddle-shaped limbs.

- *Henodus* was another turtle-like placodont. It also had a beak, which it probably used to grab molluscs from the seabed.

Nothosaurs

- **Another group of reptiles** that returned to live in the sea were the nothosaurs.

- **As its name implies**, *Nothosaurus* was a nothosaur. Its neck, tail and body were long and flexible.

- *Nothosaurus* **was** about 3 m long and its approximate weight was 200 kg.

- **Impressions** left in some *Nothosaurus* fossils show that it had webs between its toes.

- *Nothosaurus'* **jaw** had many sharp, interlocking teeth, which would have crunched up the fish and shrimps on which it fed.

- *Ceresiosaurus* was another nothosaur. Palaeontologists think it swam by swaying its body and tail from side to side, like a fish.

- *Ceresiosaurus* means 'deadly lizard'. It was bigger than *Nothosaurus* at 4 m in length and 90 kg in weight.

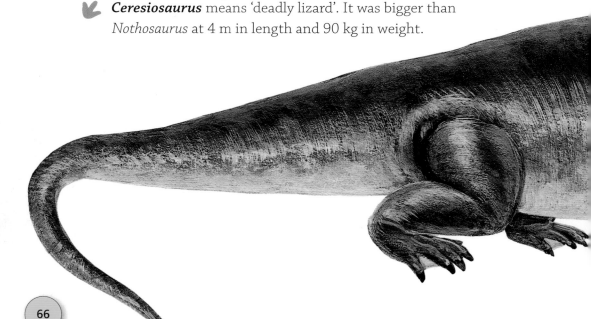

🦶 **Nothosaurs emerged** in the middle of the Triassic Period (251–200 mya), but were extinct by the end of it.

🦶 **The place left** by the extinct nothosaurs was taken by the plesiosaurs – another group of marine reptiles that were better adapted to life in the seas.

▼ Nothosaurus *was an aquatic reptile that could use its webbed feet to move over land. The long-necked nothosaurs were probably the ancestors of plesiosaurs, many of which also had long necks.*

DID YOU KNOW?
Nothosaurus had nostrils on the top of its snout, which suggests that it came to the water's surface to breathe, like crocodiles.

Plesiosaurs

Plesiosaurs were marine reptiles that were plentiful from the Late Triassic to the Late Cretaceous Periods (228–65 mya).

They were better suited to a marine lifestyle than nothosaurs or placodonts. Their limbs were fully-developed paddles, which propelled their short bodies quickly through the water.

Many plesiosaurs had a long, bendy neck. They had small heads with strong jaws and sharp teeth.

These marine reptiles had a diet that included fish, squid and probably pterosaurs (flying reptiles), which flew above the water in search of food.

The first *Plesiosaurus* fossil was discovered at Lyme Regis on the south coast of England by Mary Anning in the early 19th century. The fossil, which is in the Natural History Museum, London, is 2.3 m long.

Plesiosaurus was not a fast swimmer. It used its flipper-like limbs to move through the water but it had a weak tail that could not propel it forward very powerfully.

Elasmosaurus, the longest plesiosaur, lived in the Cretaceous Period (145–65 mya). It grew up to 14 m long and weighed up to 3 tonnes.

DID YOU KNOW?
One large pliosaur was Rhomaleosaurus, another was Liopleurodon. Both could grow up to 15 m long.

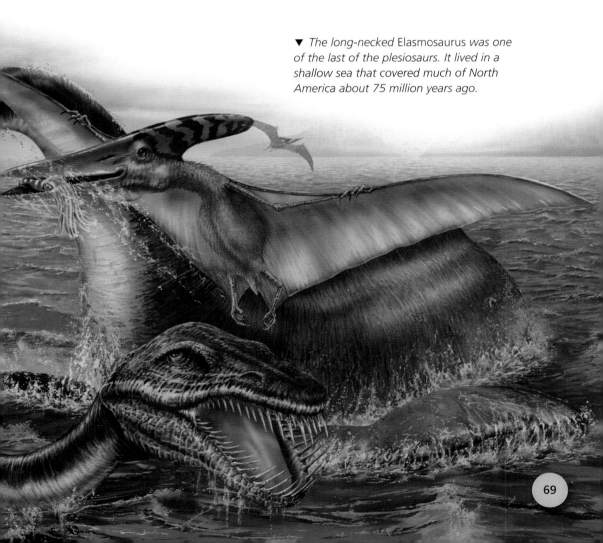

- **One group of plesiosaurs** were known as pliosaurs. They had much shorter necks and much larger heads, with huge jaws and enormous teeth.

- **Research suggests** that plesiosaurs may have caught their prey with quick, darting head movements.

▼ *The long-necked* Elasmosaurus *was one of the last of the plesiosaurs. It lived in a shallow sea that covered much of North America about 75 million years ago.*

Ichthyosaurs

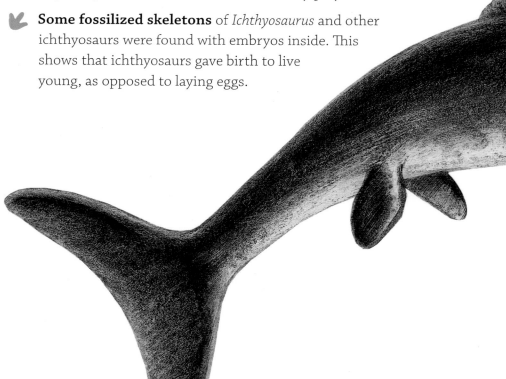

- **Ichthyosaurs looked similar** to sharks, which are fish, and to later dolphins, which are mammals. When one type of animal evolves to look like another, scientists call it convergence.

- **Unlike plesiosaurs**, which relied on their paddles to propel them forwards, ichthyosaurs swayed their tails from side to side like fish.

- **Hundreds of complete skeletons** of the ichthyosaur *Ichthyosaurus* have been discovered. This reptile could grow up to 2 m long and weighed 90 kg.

- *Ichthyosaurus* had very large ear bones. It may have been able to pick up underwater vibrations caused by prey.

- **Some fossilized skeletons** of *Ichthyosaurus* and other ichthyosaurs were found with embryos inside. This shows that ichthyosaurs gave birth to live young, as opposed to laying eggs.

- **One of the largest ichthyosaurs** was *Shonisaurus*, which was 15 m long and weighed 15 tonnes.

- **Ichthyosaurs** were plentiful in the Triassic and Jurassic Periods (257–145 mya), but became rarer in the Late Jurassic and Cretaceous Periods (145–65 mya).

- **Ichthyosaur** means 'fish lizard'.

- **Fossil hunters** have found ichthyosaur remains all over the world – in North and South America, Europe, Russia, India and Australia.

DID YOU KNOW?
The first Ichthyosaurus fossil was found in 1811 by the English fossil hunter Mary Anning. It took seven years before scientists identified the skeleton as that of a reptile.

▲ Fossils of prehistoric marine reptiles such as Ichthyosaurus *created a sensation in the early 19th century because fossil hunters discovered them before they had found any dinosaur remains.*

Mosasaurs

- **Another group** of large sea reptiles was the Mosasaurs. They appeared between 160 and 120 mya at the time when ichthyosaurs were less common.

- **Mosasaurs** were diapsid reptiles – a group that included dinosaurs and pterosaurs. All other large sea reptiles belonged to another group – the euryapsids.

- **Unlike other** giant prehistoric sea reptiles, mosasaurs have living relatives. These include monitor lizards, such as the Komodo dragon.

- **The best known mosasaur** is *Mosasaurus*, which could grow up to 10 m long and 10 tonnes in weight.

- **The huge jaws of *Mosasaurus*** were lined with cone-shaped teeth, each of which had different cutting and crushing edges. They were the most advanced teeth of any marine reptile.

- **So distinctive** are *Mosasaurus* teeth that palaeontologists have identified its tooth marks on the fossils of other animals, in particular the giant turtle *Allopleuron*.

- **The jaws of a *Mosasaurus*** were discovered in a limestone mine in Maastricht, in the Netherlands, in 1780. The fossil disappeared in 1795 when the French invaded Maastricht, but later turned up in Paris.

- **At first**, scientists thought the jaws belonged either to a prehistoric whale or a crocodile, until they decided they were a giant lizard's.

Mosasaurus means 'lizard from the River Meuse' because it was discovered in Maastricht in the Netherlands, through which the River Meuse flows.

In 1998, more than 200 years after the discovery of the first *Mosasaurus* fossil, palaeontologists discovered the remains of another *Mosasaurus* in the same location – the St Pietersburg quarry in Maastricht.

▼ Mosasaurus *was a fast swimmer. It had an enormous tail and paddle-shaped limbs, which it probably used as rudders.*

73

Rhamphorhynchoids

- **The earliest pterosaurs** (flying reptiles) were the rhamphorhynchoids. They first appeared in the Late Triassic Period (around 220 mya).

- **Rhamphorhynchoids** had long tails that ended in a diamond-shaped vane, like a rudder. Their tails gave them stability in flight, which meant they could soar and swoop effectively.

- **One of the first** rhamphorhynchoids – and first flying vertebrates – was *Peteinosaurus*.

- **Well-preserved fossils** of *Peteinosaurus* have been found near Bergamo in Italy.

- **They reveal Peteinosaurus'** sharp, cone-like teeth and suggest it ate insects that it caught in the air.

- **In contrast**, another early rhamphorhynchoid, *Eudimorphodon*, had fangs at the front of its mouth and smaller spiked ones behind. This suggests that it ate fish.

- *Dimorphodon* was a later rhamphorhynchoid from the Early Jurassic Period (208–176 mya). It had a huge head that looked a bit like a puffin's.

- *Rhamphorhynchus* was one of the last rhamphorhynchoids, appearing in the Late Jurassic Period (about 160 mya).

DID YOU KNOW?
Fossil hunters have found Rhamphorhynchus fossils alongside those of the early bird Archaeopteryx in Solnhofen, Germany.

▼ Rhamphorhynchus *had long, sharp jaws that it used to spear fish.*

▶ Dimorphodon *had a wingspan of between 1.2 and 2.5 m. Palaeontologists think that it lived and hunted along seashores and rivers.*

Pterodactyls

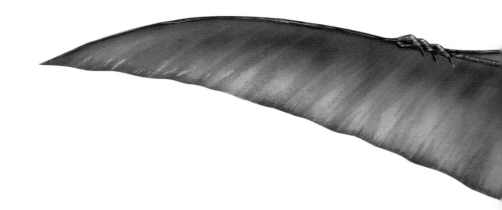

Pterodactyls are a later group of pterosaurs (flying reptiles) than the rhamphorhynchoids.

They lived in the Late Jurassic through to the Late Cretaceous Periods (161–65 mya).

Although pterodactyls lacked the long, stabilizing tail of rhamphorhynchoids, they were more effective fliers and able to make quicker turns in the air.

These later pterosaurs were also much lighter than rhamphorhynchoids because their bones were hollow.

The pterodactyl *Pterodactylus* and the rhamphorhynchoid *Rhamphorhynchus* were roughly the same size, but *Pterodactylus* weighed between 1–5 kg, while *Rhamphorhynchus* was heavier at about 10 kg.

Some of the largest pterodactyls, such as *Pteranodon*, appeared in the Late Cretaceous Period and had a wingspan of 7 m.

- **Unlike earlier flying reptiles**, *Pteranodon* had no teeth. Instead, it used its long, thin beak to scoop up fish.

- **At the bottom** of its mouth *Pteranodon* had a pelican-like pouch – it probably used this to store fish before swallowing them.

- ***Pteranodon*** weighed about 16 kg. This was heavier than earlier pterodactyls and suggests it was probably a glider rather than an active flyer.

- **A long crest** on *Pteranodon's* head may have worked as a rudder during flight.

▲ *One of the largest flying creatures of all time was* Pteranodon. *This great reptile had a wingspan of up to 9 m. It lived about 75 million years ago, feeding on fish that lived in the shallow seas that then covered much of North America.*

Dinosaurs

Ancestors

 Experts have many opinions about which group (or groups) of reptiles were the ancestors of the dinosaurs.

Very early dinosaurs walked and ran on their strong back limbs, so their ancestors probably did the same.

The thecodonts, or 'socket-toothed', group of reptiles may have been the ancestors of the dinosaurs.

A thecodont's teeth grew from roots fixed into pit-like sockets in the jaw bone, as in dinosaurs.

Some thecodonts resembled sturdy lizards. Others evolved into true crocodiles, which are still around today.

The ornithosuchian thecodonts became small, upright creatures with long back legs and long tails.

The smaller thecodonts included *Euparkeria*, at about 60 cm long, and *Lagosuchus*, at about 30 cm long.

Euparkeria and *Lagosuchus* were fast-moving creatures that used their sharp claws and teeth to catch insects.

DID YOU KNOW?
Creatures similar to Euparkeria or Lagosuchus may have given rise to the first dinosaurs.

▶ Modern-day crocodiles and alligators belong to the same reptile group, known as archosaurs, that the dinosaurs belonged to. This means they both have the same ancestors, which date back more than 230 million years.

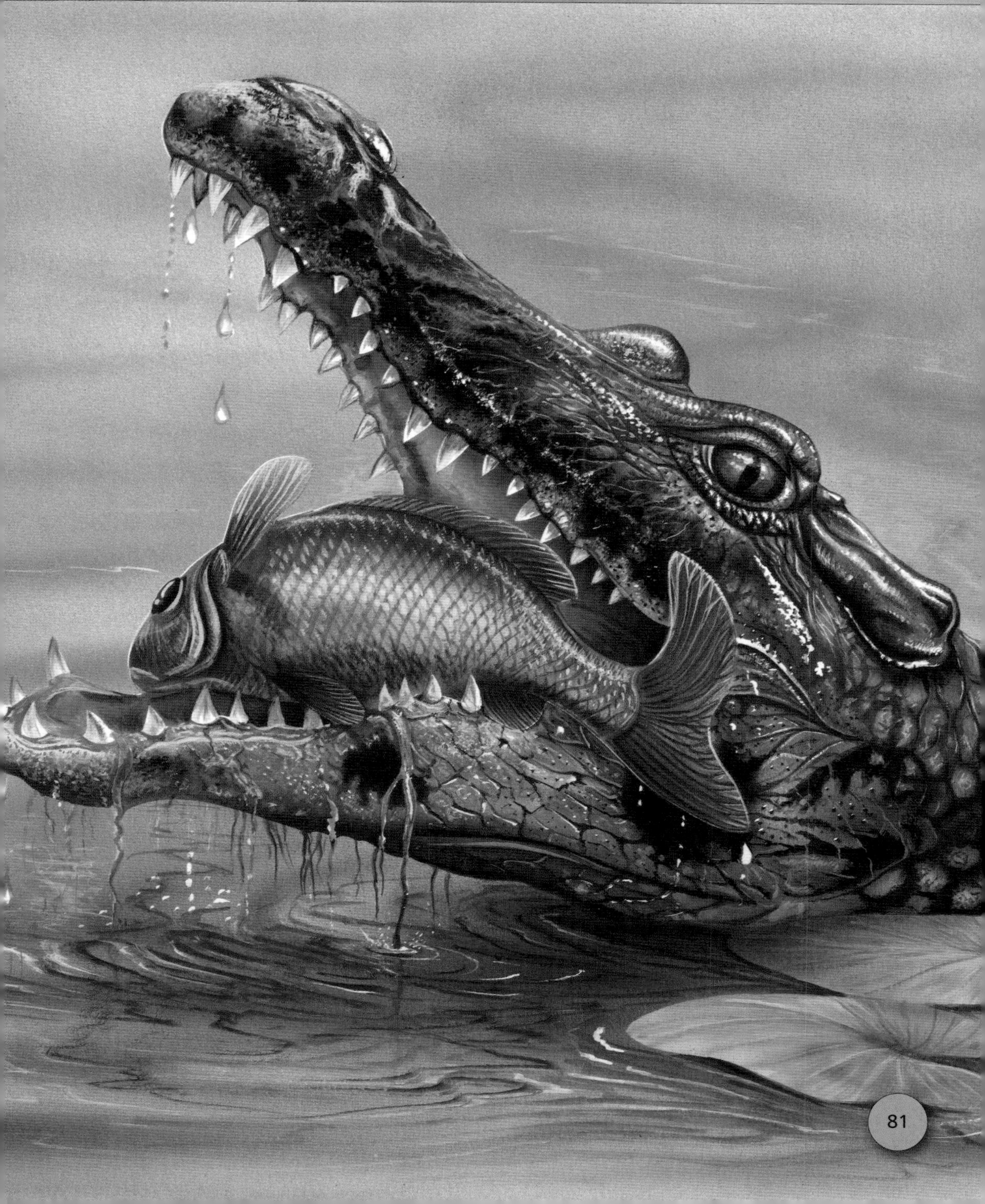

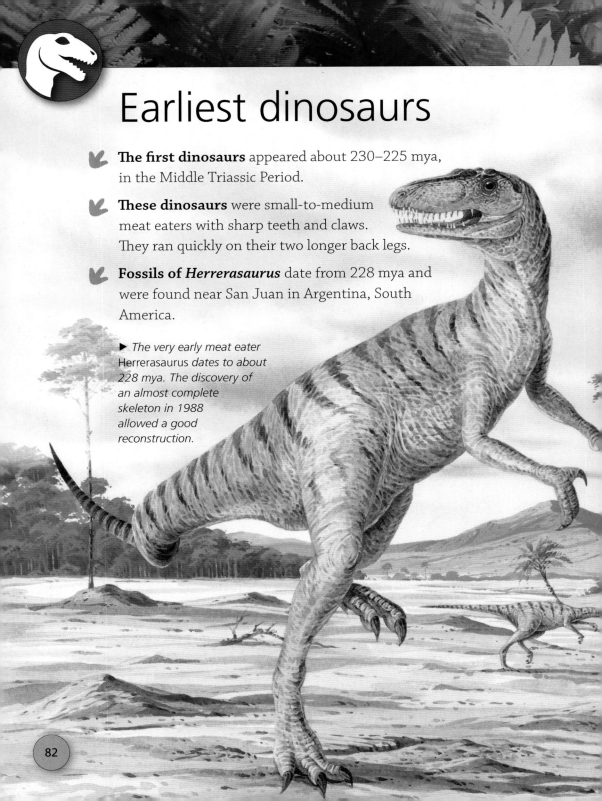

Earliest dinosaurs

- **The first dinosaurs** appeared about 230–225 mya, in the Middle Triassic Period.

- **These dinosaurs** were small-to-medium meat eaters with sharp teeth and claws. They ran quickly on their two longer back legs.

- **Fossils of *Herrerasaurus*** date from 228 mya and were found near San Juan in Argentina, South America.

▶ The very early meat eater Herrerasaurus *dates to about 228 mya. The discovery of an almost complete skeleton in 1988 allowed a good reconstruction.*

- *Herrerasaurus* was about 3 m in total length, and probably weighed some 90 kg.

- **At about the same time** and in the same place as *Herrerasaurus*, there lived a similar-shaped dinosaur named *Eoraptor*, which was only 1.5 m long.

- **The name *Eoraptor*** means 'dawn plunderer' or 'early thief'.

- *Staurikosaurus* was a meat eater similar to *Herrerasaurus*. It is known to have lived about the same time, in present-day Brazil, South America.

- *Procompsognathus* was another early meat eater. It lived in the Late Triassic Period in Germany.

- *Pisanosaurus* lived in Argentina in the Late Triassic Period, and was only one metre long. It may have been a plant eater.

DID YOU KNOW?

Eoraptor and Herrerasaurus hunted small animals such as lizards, insects and lizard-like reptiles.

Coelophysis

Coelophysis was a small, agile dinosaur that lived early in the Age of Dinosaurs, about 220 mya.

A huge collection of *Coelophysis* fossils was found in the 1940s, at a place called Ghost Ranch, New Mexico, USA.

▶ Coelophysis *would have stood almost waist-high to a person as it darted about on its long back legs.*

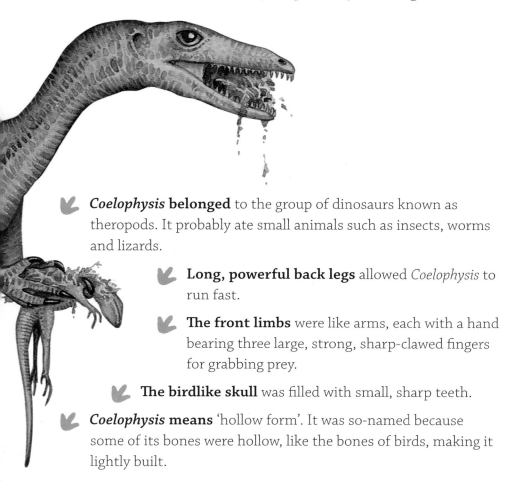

- **Hundreds** of *Coelophysis* were preserved together at Ghost Ranch – possibly a herd that drowned in a flood.

- *Coelophysis* **was almost** 3 m in total length. Its slim, lightweight build meant that it probably weighed only 25–28 kg.

- *Coelophysis* **belonged** to the group of dinosaurs known as theropods. It probably ate small animals such as insects, worms and lizards.

- **Long, powerful back legs** allowed *Coelophysis* to run fast.

- **The front limbs** were like arms, each with a hand bearing three large, strong, sharp-clawed fingers for grabbing prey.

- **The birdlike skull** was filled with small, sharp teeth.

- *Coelophysis* **means** 'hollow form'. It was so-named because some of its bones were hollow, like the bones of birds, making it lightly built.

Dilophosaurus

- *Dilophosaurus* **was** a large meat-eating theropod dinosaur that lived about 200 mya.

- **Fossils** of *Dilophosaurus* were found in Arizona, USA, and possibly Yunnan, China.

- **The fossils** in Arizona were discovered by Jesse Williams, a Navajo Native American, in 1942.

- **Studying the fossils** proved very difficult, and the dinosaur was not given its official name until 1970.

- *Dilophosaurus* **measured** about 6 m from its nose to the end of its very long tail.

- **The name** *Dilophosaurus* means 'two ridged reptile', from the two thin, rounded, bony crests on its head, each shaped like half a dinner plate.

- **The crests** were too thin and fragile to be used as weapons for head-butting.

- **Brightly coloured skin** may have covered the head crests, as a visual display to rivals or enemies.

▶ Dilophosaurus *is the first big, powerful, predatory dinosaur known from fossil evidence.*

DID YOU KNOW?

Dilophosaurus probably weighed about 500 kg – as much as the biggest polar bears today.

Eustreptospondylus

Eustreptospondylus was a large meat eater that lived in present-day Oxfordshire and Buckinghamshire, in England. It lived about 165 mya.

In the 1850s, a fairly complete skeleton of a young *Eustreptospondylus* was found near Wolvercote, Oxford, but was named as *Megalosaurus*, the only other big meat eater known from the region.

In 1964, British fossil expert Alick Walker showed that the Wolvercote dinosaur was not *Megalosaurus*, and gave it a new name, *Eustreptospondylus*.

A full-grown *Eustreptospondylus* measured about 7 m in length and is estimated to have weighed 200–250 kg.

In its enormous mouth, *Eustreptospondylus* had a great number of small, sharp teeth.

Eustreptospondylus may have hunted sauropods such as *Cetiosaurus* and stegosaurs, two groups of dinosaurs that roamed the region at the time.

DID YOU KNOW?
Eustreptospondylus means 'well-curved backbone'. This is due to the arrangement of its spine as seen in its fossils.

▼ Eustreptospondylus *weighed about the same as a very large lion today, and was doubtless just as deadly.*

Baryonyx

- *Baryonyx* **was** a large meat-eating dinosaur that lived about 120 mya.

- **The first fossil find** of *Baryonyx* was its huge thumb claw, discovered in Surrey, England, in 1983.

- **The total length** of *Baryonyx* was 10–11 m.

- *Baryonyx* **had** a slim shape and long, narrow tail, and probably weighed less than 2 tonnes.

- **The snout was unusual** for a meat-eating dinosaur because it was very long and narrow – similar to today's slim-snouted crocodiles.

- **The teeth were long** and slim, especially at the front of the mouth.

- **The general similarities** between *Baryonyx* and a crocodile suggest that *Baryonyx* may have been a fish eater.

- **It may have lurked** in swamps or close to rivers, darting its head forward on its long, flexible neck to snatch fish.

- **The massive thumb claw**, which measured 35 cm in length, may have been used to hook fish or amphibians from the water.

▲ *Fossils of* Baryonyx *were found with the remains of fish scales, suggesting this dinosaur was a semi-aquatic fish catcher.*

Allosaurus

- **A big meat eater**, *Allosaurus* was almost the same size as *Tyrannosaurus*. It lived about 155–135 mya, during the Late Jurassic and Early Cretaceous Periods.

- *Allosaurus* **was** about 11–12 m in total length and its weight is variously estimated at 1.5–4 tonnes.

- **The head** was almost one metre in length, but its skull was light, with large gaps, or 'windows', that would have been covered by muscle and skin.

- **Not only** could *Allosaurus* open its jaws in a huge gape, it could also flex them so that the whole mouth became wider, for an even bigger bite.

- **Most** *Allosaurus* **fossils** come from the states in the American Midwest.

- *Allosaurus* may have hunted giant sauropod dinosaurs such as *Diplodocus*, *Camarasaurus* and *Brachiosaurus*.

- **Fossils of** *Allosaurus* were identified in Africa, and a smaller 'dwarf' version was found in Australia.

DID YOU KNOW?

The remains of 60 Allosaurus were found in the Cleveland-Lloyd Dinosaur Quarry, Utah, USA.

▲ Allosaurus *almost rivalled*
Tyrannosaurus *in size, but lived*
70 million years earlier.

Carnotaurus

- **The big, powerful, meat-eating** *Carnotaurus* belongs to the theropod dinosaur group. It lived about 100 mya.

- ***Carnotaurus* fossils** come mainly from the Chubut region of Argentina, South America.

- **A medium-sized dinosaur,** *Carnotaurus* was about 7.5 m in total length and weighed up to one tonne.

- **The skull** was relatively tall from top to bottom and short from front to back, compared to other meat eaters such as *Allosaurus* and *Tyrannosaurus*. This gave *Carnotaurus* a snub-snouted appearance.

- **The name *Carnotaurus*** means 'meat-eating bull', referring partly to its bull-like face.

- ***Carnotaurus* had** two cone-shaped bony crests, or 'horns', one above each eye.

- **Rows of extra-large scales**, like small lumps, ran along *Carnotaurus* from head to tail.

- **Like *Tyrannosaurus*,** *Carnotaurus* had small front limbs that could not reach its mouth and may have had no use.

- ***Carnotaurus* probably ate** plant-eating dinosaurs such as *Chubutisaurus*, although its teeth and jaws were not especially big or strong.

◄ *The fossils of* Carnotaurus *were first discovered in 1985.*

Tyrannosaurus

Tyrannosaurus **is not only** one of the most famous dinosaurs, it is also one about which a great deal is known. Several discoveries have revealed fossilized bones, teeth and whole skeletons.

Tyrannosaurus **lived** at the very end of the Age of Dinosaurs, about 70–65 mya.

Its full name is *Tyrannosaurus rex*, which means 'king of the tyrant reptiles'.

The head was 1.2 m long and had more than 50 dagger-like teeth, some longer than 15 cm.

Tyrannosaurus **fossils** have been found at many sites in North America, including Alberta and Saskatchewan in Canada, and Colorado, Wyoming, Montana and New Mexico in the USA.

The arms and hands of *Tyrannosaurus* were so small that they could not pass food to its mouth, and may have had no use at all.

Recent fossil finds of a group of *Tyrannosaurus* include youngsters, suggesting that they may have lived as families in small herds.

Tyrannosaurus may have been an active hunter, pounding along with long strides after its fleeing prey, or it may have been a skulking scavenger that ambushed old and sickly victims.

Thick, heavy, muscular base to tail

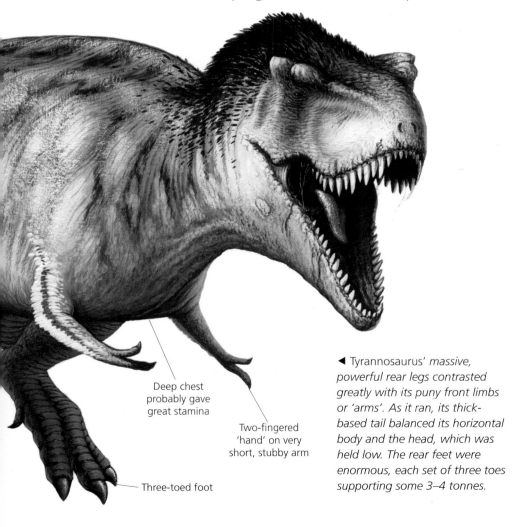

Until the 1990s, *Tyrannosaurus* was known as the biggest meat-eating dinosaur, and the biggest meat-eating animal ever to walk the Earth, but its size record was broken by *Giganotosaurus* and then *Spinosaurus*.

Deep chest probably gave great stamina

Two-fingered 'hand' on very short, stubby arm

Three-toed foot

◄ Tyrannosaurus' *massive, powerful rear legs contrasted greatly with its puny front limbs or 'arms'. As it ran, its thick-based tail balanced its horizontal body and the head, which was held low. The rear feet were enormous, each set of three toes supporting some 3–4 tonnes.*

Ornitholestes

- **Ornitholestes was** a smallish meat eater from the coelurosaur dinosaur group. It lived about 150 mya, at the same time as the first birds.

- **The name *Ornitholestes*** means 'bird robber' – experts who studied its fossils in the early 1900s imagined it chasing and killing the earliest birds.

- **The home of *Ornitholestes*** was actually in present-day Wyoming in the USA – a continent away from the earliest birds in Europe.

- **Only one specimen** of *Ornitholestes* has been found, along with parts of a hand at another site.

- **Ornitholestes was** about 2 m long from nose to tail and probably weighed about 12–15 kg.

DID YOU KNOW?

According to some experts, Ornitholestes may have had a slight ridge or crest on its nose. Other experts disagree.

The **teeth were small** and well-spaced, but also slim and sharp, well suited to grabbing small animals for food.

***Ornitholestes* had** very strong arms and hands with powerful fingers and long claws – ideal for grabbing baby dinosaurs newly hatched from their eggs.

▼ Ornitholestes *relied on speed and its good senses of sight and smell for survival.*

99

Oviraptor

🐾 *Oviraptor* **was** an unusual meat eater from the theropod dinosaur group. It lived during the Late Cretaceous Period about 85–75 mya.

🐾 **Its fossils** were found in the Omnogov region of the Gobi Desert in Central Asia.

🐾 **From beak to tail**, *Oviraptor* was about 2 m long.

🐾 **It was named** 'egg thief' because the first of its fossils was found lying among the broken eggs of what was thought to be the dinosaur *Protoceratops*.

🐾 *Oviraptor* **had no teeth**. Instead, it had a strong, curved beak, like that of a parrot or eagle.

🐾 **On its forehead**, *Oviraptor* had a tall, rounded piece of bone, like a crest or helmet, sticking up in front of its eyes.

🐾 *Oviraptor's* **head crest** resembled that of today's flightless bird, the cassowary.

🐾 *Oviraptor* **may have** eaten eggs, or cracked open shellfish with its powerful beak.

DID YOU KNOW?
Oviraptor had two bony spikes inside its mouth that it may have used to crack eggs when it closed its jaws.

► Oviraptor's *unusual features included its parrot-like beak.*

Smallest dinosaurs

- **One of the smallest dinosaurs** was *Compsognathus*, which lived during the Late Jurassic Period, 155–150 mya.

- **Its fossils** come from Europe, especially southern Germany and southeastern France.

- ***Compsognathus*** was about one metre in length and may have weighed less than 3 kg.

- **It had small teeth** that were sharp and curved and it probably darted through the undergrowth after insects, spiders, worms and similar small prey.

▶ *About half of the length of* Compsognathus *was its tail.*

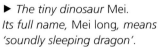

▶ *The tiny dinosaur* Mei. *Its full name,* Mei long, *means 'soundly sleeping dragon'.*

Discovered in 2004 in China, *Mei* was just 52 cm long. It is not only one of the smallest dinosaurs ever found, it also has the shortest dinosaur name of just three letters.

Mei **was fossilized** in a spookily birdlike position with its head bent to one side under its front limb or 'arm', just like a bird tucks its head under its wing when asleep.

The smallest fossil dinosaur specimens found to date are of *Mussaurus*, which means 'mouse reptile'. The fossils were of babies, just 20 cm long, newly hatched from eggs. The babies would have grown into adults measuring 3 m in length.

Two other small dinosaurs were the 90-cm-long *Heterodontosaurus* and the one-metre-long *Lesothosaurus*.

Pack hunters

- **Dinosaurs were reptiles**, but no reptiles today hunt in packs in which members co-operate with each other.

- **Certain types of crocodiles** and alligators come together to feed where prey is abundant, but they do not co-ordinate their attacks.

- **Fossil evidence** suggests that several kinds of meat-eating dinosaurs hunted in groups or packs.

- **Sometimes the fossils** of several individuals of the same type of dinosaur have been found in one place, suggesting the dinosaurs were pack animals.

- **The fossil bones** of some plant-eating dinosaurs have been found with many tooth marks on them, apparently made by different-sized predators, which may have hunted in packs.

- *Tyrannosaurus* may have been a pack hunter.

- **In southwest Montana, USA**, the remains of three or four *Deinonychus* were found near the fossils of a much larger plant eater named *Tenontosaurus*.

- **One *Deinonychus*** probably would not have attacked a full-grown *Tenontosaurus*, but a group of three or four might have.

▼ *Small predatory dinosaurs such as* Troodon *may have gathered in groups to chase prey or scavenge.*

Raptors

- **'Raptors' is a nickname** for the dromaeosaur group. It is variously said to mean 'plunderer', 'thief' or 'hunter' (birds of prey are also called raptors).

- **Dromaeosaurs were** medium-sized, powerful, agile, meat-eating dinosaurs that lived mainly about 110–65 mya.

- **Most dromaeosaurs** were 1.5–3 m from nose to tail, weighed 20–60 kg, and stood 1–2 m tall.

- ***Velociraptor* lived** 75–70 mya, in what is now the barren scrub and desert of Mongolia in Central Asia.

- **Like other raptors**, *Velociraptor* probably ran fast and could leap great distances on its powerful back legs.

- **The dromaeosaurs** are named after the 1.8-m-long *Dromaeosaurus* from North America – one of the least known of the group, from very few fossil finds.

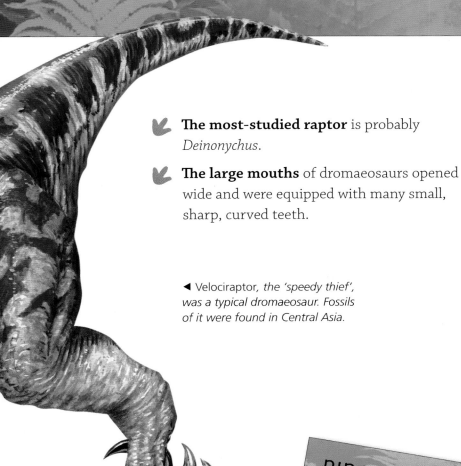

- **The most-studied raptor** is probably *Deinonychus*.

- **The large mouths** of dromaeosaurs opened wide and were equipped with many small, sharp, curved teeth.

◄ Velociraptor, *the 'speedy thief',
was a typical dromaeosaur. Fossils
of it were found in Central Asia.*

DID YOU KNOW?
On each foot, a dromaeosaur had a large, curved claw that it could swing in an arc to slash through its victim's flesh.

107

Deinonychus

- *Deinonychus* **is one** of the best known raptors.

- **It thrived** in the Middle Cretaceous Period, about 115–100 mya.

- **Fossils of** *Deinonychus* come from the American Midwest, mainly from Montana and Wyoming.

- *Deinonychus* **was about** 3 m long from nose to tail and weighed 60–70 kg, about the same as an adult human.

- **When remains of** *Deinonychus* were dug up and studied in the 1960s, they exploded the myth that dinosaurs were slow, small-brained and stupid.

- **Powerful, speedy and agile**, *Deinonychus* may have hunted in packs, like today's lions and wolves.

- **It had large hands** with three powerful fingers, each tipped with a dangerous sharp claw.

- *Deinonychus* **also had** the massive, scythelike claw, typical of the raptor group.

- **The tail** was stiff and could not be swished.

- *Deinonychus* **and other** similar dromaeosaurs, such as *Velociraptor*, were the basis for the cunning and terrifying raptors of the *Jurassic Park* films.

▶ Deinonychus *may have attacked prey much larger than itself.*

Archaeopteryx

- **The earliest known bird** for which there is good fossil evidence, and which lived during the Age of Dinosaurs, is known as *Archaeopteryx*, meaning 'ancient wing'.

- *Archaeopteryx* **lived** in Europe during the Late Jurassic Period, about 155–150 mya.

- **At about 60 cm long** from nose to tail, *Archaeopteryx* was about the size of a large crow.

- *Archaeopteryx* **resembled** a small, meat-eating dinosaur in many of its features, such as the teeth in its long, beaklike mouth, and its long, bony tail.

- **In 1951**, a fossilized part-skeleton was identified as a small dinosaur similar to *Compsognathus*, but in the 1970s it was re-studied and named *Archaeopteryx* – showing how similar the two creatures were.

- **Three clawed fingers** grew halfway along the front of each of *Archaeopteryx's* wing-shaped front limbs.

- **The flying muscles** were anchored to its large breastbone.

- *Archaeopteryx* **probably flew**, but not as fast or as skillfully as today's birds.

DID YOU KNOW?

Archaeopteryx was covered with feathers that had the same detailed designs found in those covering flying birds today.

Long tail with tail backbones

Flight feathers suited to agile manoeuvres in the air

▼ Archaeopteryx *could probably glide, swoop and turn as it pursued flying prey such as dragonflies. However, its long, strong legs suggest that it was also an able walker and runner, so it may have chased victims such as baby lizards and cockroaches on the ground.*

Dino birds

🐾 **Fossils found** during the last 20 years show that some dinosaurs may have been covered with feathers or fur.

🐾 *Sinosauropteryx* was a small, one-metre-long meat eater that lived 135 mya in China.

🐾 **Fossils of *Sinosauropteryx*** show that parts of its body were covered not with the usual reptile scales, but with feathers.

🐾 **The overall shape** of *Sinosauropteryx* shows that, despite being feathered, it could not fly.

🐾 **The feathers** may have been for camouflage, for visual display, or to keep it warm – suggesting it was warm-blooded.

🐾 **Fossils of *Avimimus*** come from China and Mongolia, and date from 85–82 mya.

🐾 **The fossil arm bones** have small ridges that are the same size and shape as the ridges on birds' wing bones, where feathers attach.

🐾 **The 1.5-m-long *Avimimus*** had a mouth shaped like a bird's beak for pecking at food.

Many scientists today believe that birds are descended from small meat-eating dinosaurs called maniraptorans, such as *Troodon*.

If this is so, the modern way of classifying or grouping animals, called cladistics, means that birds are a sub group of dinosaurs, not a separate group. That would mean that dinosaurs are alive today – in the form of birds.

▲ Avimimus *may have evolved feathers for warmth or camouflage.*

113

Ostrich dinosaurs

🦶 **'Ostrich dinosaurs'** is the common name of the ornithomimosaurs, because of their resemblance to today's largest bird – the flightless ostrich.

🦶 **These dinosaurs** were tall and slim, with two long, powerful back legs for running very fast.

🦶 **The front limbs** were like strong arms, with grasping fingers tipped by sharp claws.

🦶 **The eyes were large** and set high on the head.

🦶 **The toothless mouth** was similar to the long, slim beak of a bird.

🦶 **Ostrich dinosaurs** lived towards the end of the Cretaceous Period, about 100–65 mya, in North America and Asia.

🦶 **Fossils of** the ostrich dinosaur *Struthiomimus* from Alberta, Canada, suggest it was almost 4 m in total length and stood about 2 m tall – the same height as a modern ostrich.

🦶 **The ostrich dinosaur** *Gallimimus* was almost 6 m long and stood nearly 3 m high.

Ostrich dinosaurs probably ate seeds, fruits and other plant material, as well as small animals such as worms and lizards, which they may have grasped with their powerful clawed hands.

Other ostrich dinosaurs included *Dromiceiomimus*, at 3–4 m long, and the slightly bigger *Ornithomimus*.

▼ Ornithomimus *could reach speeds of 80 km/h when running. It had strong muscles in its hips and legs enabling it to take long, quick strides.*

Herbivores

Hundreds of kinds of dinosaurs were herbivores, or plant eaters. As time passed, the plants available for them to eat changed or evolved.

Early in the Age of Dinosaurs, during the Triassic Period, the main plants for dinosaurs to eat were conifer trees, ginkgoes, cycads and the smaller seed ferns, ferns, horsetails and club mosses.

A few cycads are still found today. They resemble palm trees, with umbrella-like crowns of long green fronds on top of tall, unbranched, trunklike stems.

In the Triassic Period, only prosauropod dinosaurs were big enough or had necks long enough to reach tall cycad fronds or ginkgo leaves.

In the Jurassic Period, tall conifers such as redwoods and 'monkey puzzle' trees became common.

The huge, long-necked sauropods of the Jurassic Period may have been able to reach high into tall conifer trees to rake off their needles.

In the Middle Cretaceous Period, a new type of plant food appeared – the flowering plants.

By the end of the Cretaceous Period there were many flowering trees and shrubs, such as magnolias, maples and walnuts.

These new plants meant that many new kinds of herbivorous dinosaurs evolved to eat them.

▼ *During the warm, damp Jurassic Period, plants grew in most areas, covering land that previously had been barren. Massive plant eaters such as* Barosaurus *thrived on the fronds, needles and leaves of towering tree ferns, ginkgoes and conifers.*

Barosaurus was 26 m long and weighed 25–30 tonnes

117

Prosauropods

- **The first big dinosaurs** were the prosauropods. They lived 230–180 mya.

- **They were plant eaters**, with small heads, long necks and tails, wide bodies and four sturdy limbs.

- **One of the first prosauropods** was *Plateosaurus*, which lived in Europe. Earlier prosauropods lived in Madagascar, 225 mya.

- *Plateosaurus* **walked** on all fours, but may have reared up on its back legs to reach leaves. It was up to 8 m long, and weighed about one tonne.

- **Another prosauropod** was *Riojasaurus*. Its fossils are 218 million years old, and come from Argentina.

- *Riojasaurus* **was 10 m long** and weighed about 2 tonnes.

More than 20 fossil skeletons of the prosauropod *Sellosaurus* have been found in Europe, dating from 225–220 million years ago.

Lufengosaurus was an early Jurassic prosauropod from China, measuring about 6 m in length. It was the first complete dinosaur skeleton to be restored in that country.

The sauropods followed the prosauropods and were even bigger, but had the same basic body shape, with long necks and tails.

▼ Riojasaurus *was South America's first big dinosaur.*

119

Plateosaurus

- **The name *Plateosaurus*** means 'flat reptile', and it appeared around 220 mya.

- **Groups of *Plateosaurus*** have been found at various sites, including one in Germany and one in France.

- ***Plateosaurus* had** jagged teeth for chewing plants.

- **Its flexible, clawed fingers** may have been used to pull branches of food to its mouth.

◄ Plateosaurus *may have been able to reach leaves 2–3 m above the ground.*

- *Plateosaurus* **could bend** its fingers 'backwards', allowing it to walk on its hands and fingers, in the same posture as its feet and toes.

- **The thumbs** had large, sharp claws, perhaps used to jab and stab enemies.

- **Fossil experts** once thought that *Plateosaurus* dragged its tail as it walked.

- **Experts today** think that *Plateosaurus* carried its tail off the ground to balance its head, neck and the front part of its body.

- *Plateosaurus* was one of the earliest dinosaurs to be officially named, in 1837, even before the term 'dinosaur' had been invented.

Massospondylus

- *Massospondylus* **was** a medium-sized plant eater belonging to the group known as the prosauropods.

- **Africa and perhaps North America** were home to *Massospondylus*, about 200 mya.

- **In total**, *Massospondylus* was about 5 m long, with almost half of this length being its tail.

- **The rear legs** of *Massospondylus* were bigger and stronger than its front legs, so it may have reared up to reach high-up food.

- **The name** *Massospondylus* means 'huge backbone'.

- **Fossils of more than 80** *Massospondylus* have been found, making it one of the best-studied dinosaurs.

- *Massospondylus* had a tiny head compared to its body, so it must have spent hours each day gathering enough food to survive.

- **The front teeth** of *Massospondylus* were large and strong with ridged edges.

The cheek teeth were too small and weak to chew large amounts of food, so perhaps food was mashed in the dinosaur's stomach.

In the 1980s, some scientists suggested that *Massospondylus* may have been a meat eater, partly due to its ridged front teeth.

▶ Massospondylus *probably spent most of its time eating to fuel its bulky body.*

123

Anchisaurus

- *Anchisaurus* **was** an early sauropod dinosaur.

- **Although officially named** as a dinosaur in 1912, *Anchisaurus* had in fact been discovered almost 100 years earlier.

- *Anchisaurus* **was very small** and slim compared to other sauropods, with a body about the size of a large dog.

- **Fossils of** *Anchisaurus* date from the Early Jurassic Period.

- **The remains of** *Anchisaurus* were found in Connecticut and Massachusetts, eastern USA, and in southern Africa.

- **With its small, serrated teeth,** *Anchisaurus* probably bit off the soft leaves of low-growing plants.

- **To reach leaves** on higher branches, *Anchisaurus* may have been able to rear up on its back legs.

- *Anchisaurus* had a large, curved claw on each thumb.

- **The thumb claws** may have been used as hooks to pull leafy branches towards the mouth, or as weapons for lashing out at enemies and inflicting wounds.

▼ Anchisaurus *was about 2.25 m long. Its name means 'near lizard'.*

DID YOU KNOW?
Remains of Anchisaurus were the first fossils of a dinosaur to be discovered in North America in 1818.

Biggest dinosaurs

- **Dinosaurs can be** measured by length and height, but 'biggest' usually means heaviest or bulkiest.

- **The sauropod dinosaurs** of the Late Jurassic and Early–Mid Cretaceous Periods were the biggest animals to walk on Earth, as far as we know.

- **However, today's whales**, and maybe the huge sea reptiles (pliosaurs) of the Dinosaur Age, rival them in size.

Long neck for reaching high leaves

▶ Seismosaurus *is known from just a few fossils.*

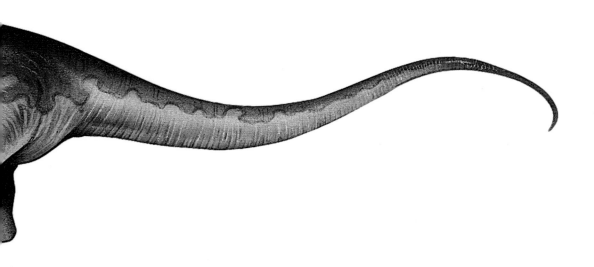

- **For any dinosaur**, enough fossils must be found for scientists to be sure it is a distinct type so they can give it a scientific name. They must also be able to estimate its size. With some giant dinosaurs, not enough fossils have been found.

- **Remains of *Supersaurus*** found in Colorado, USA, suggest a dinosaur similar to *Diplodocus*, but perhaps even longer, at 35 m.

- ***Seismosaurus* fossils** found in 1991 in the USA may belong to a 40-m-long sauropod.

- ***Ultrasaurus*** fossils found in South Korea suggest a dinosaur similar to *Brachiosaurus*, but smaller.

- ***Argentinosaurus***, from South America, is known from a few fossils, mainly backbones, found in the early 1990s. It may have weighed 100 tonnes or more.

Sauropods

- **Sauropods were the biggest** dinosaurs of all. They lived mainly during the Jurassic Period, around 208–144 mya.

- **These huge plant eaters** had tiny heads, very long necks and tails, huge, bulging bodies and massive legs, similar to those of an elephant, but much bigger.

- **Sauropods included** the well known *Mamenchisaurus*, *Cetiosaurus*, *Diplodocus*, *Brachiosaurus* and *Apatosaurus*.

- ***Rebbachisaurus* fossils** were found in Morocco, Tunisia and Algeria. It lived 120 mya.

- ***Cetiosaurus* was** about 18 m long and weighed 30 tonnes.

The first fossils of *Cetiosaurus* were found in Oxfordshire, England, in the 1830s. It was the first sauropod to be given an official name, in 1841 – the year before the term 'dinosaur' was invented.

Cetiosaurus, or 'whale reptile', was so-named because French fossil expert Georges Cuvier thought that its giant backbones came from a prehistoric whale.

▶ *Sauropods such as* Apatosaurus *could perhaps browse in tree tops.*

Brachiosaurus

- **Relatively complete** fossil remains exist of the sauropod *Brachiosaurus*. It lived about 150 mya, and may have survived until 115 mya.

- **At 25 m in length** from nose to tail, *Brachiosaurus* was not one of the longest dinosaurs, but it was one of the heaviest. Its weight has been estimated between 30–75 tonnes.

- ***Brachiosaurus* fossils** have been found in North America, east and north Africa, and also possibly southern Europe.

- **The name *Brachiosaurus*** means 'arm reptile' – it was so-named because of its massive front legs.

- **With its huge front legs** and long neck, *Brachiosaurus* could perhaps reach food more than 13 m from the ground.

Its teeth were small and chisel-shaped for snipping leaves from trees.

Its nostrils were positioned high on its head.

◀ Brachiosaurus *had similar body proportions to a giraffe, but was more than twice as tall and 50 times heavier.*

Camarasaurus

- **Camarasaurus** was a giant plant-eating sauropod that lived during the Late Jurassic Period, about 155–150 mya.

- **It is one of** the best known of all big dinosaurs, because so many almost-complete fossil skeletons have been found.

◄ Compared to other sauropods, Camarasaurus had a short neck and tail.

- **Famous American fossil hunter** Edward Drinker Cope gave *Camarasaurus* its name in 1877.

- **The name means** 'chambered reptile', because its backbones, or vertebrae, had large, scoop-shaped spaces in them, making them lighter.

- ***Camarasaurus*** was about 18 m long and had a very bulky, powerful body and legs.

- **North America**, Europe and Africa were home to *Camarasaurus*.

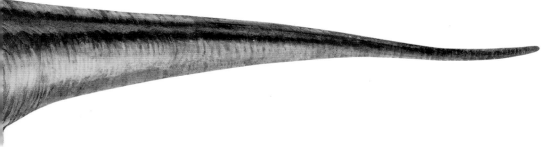

- **A large, short-snouted head**, similar to that of *Brachiosaurus*, characterized *Camarasaurus*.

- **A fossil skeleton** of a young *Camarasaurus* was uncovered in the 1920s, and had nearly every bone in its body lying in the correct position, as they were when the dinosaur was alive – an amazingly rare find.

Diplodocus

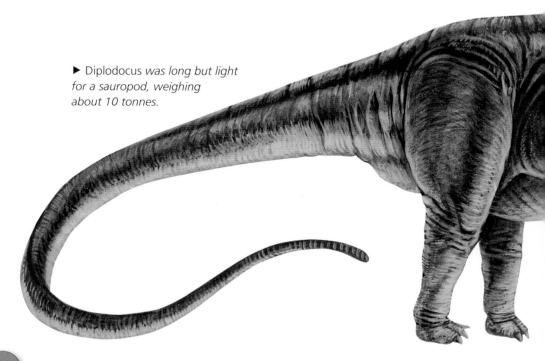

- *Diplodocus* was a huge plant-eating sauropod that lived during the Late Jurassic Period, about 155–145 mya.

- **The first discovery** of *Diplodocus* fossils was in 1877, near Canyon City, Colorado, USA.

- **The main fossils** were found in the USA, in Colorado, Utah and Wyoming.

- **At an incredible 27 m** or more in length, *Diplodocus* is one of the longest dinosaurs known.

- *Diplodocus* **probably** swung its tiny head on its enormous neck to reach fronds and foliage in the trees.

▶ Diplodocus *was long but light for a sauropod, weighing about 10 tonnes.*

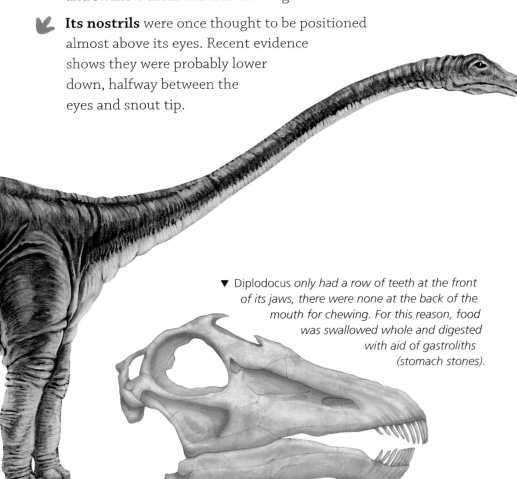

- **Its teeth** were slim rods that formed a comblike fringe around the front of its mouth.

- *Diplodocus* **may have** used these teeth to strip leaves from twigs and swallow them without chewing.

- **Its nostrils** were once thought to be positioned almost above its eyes. Recent evidence shows they were probably lower down, halfway between the eyes and snout tip.

▼ Diplodocus *only had a row of teeth at the front of its jaws, there were none at the back of the mouth for chewing. For this reason, food was swallowed whole and digested with aid of gastroliths (stomach stones).*

135

Mamenchisaurus

- **A massive plant-eating dinosaur**, *Mamenchisaurus* was similar in appearance to *Diplodocus*.

- **It lived** during the late Jurassic Period, from 160–140 mya.

- **This huge dinosaur** measured about 25 m from nose to tail. Its weight has been estimated at 20–35 tonnes.

- **At up to 15 m**, *Mamenchisaurus* had one of the longest necks of any dinosaur. The neck had up to 19 vertebrae, or neckbones – more than almost any other dinosaur.

- **The remains** of *Mamenchisaurus* were found in China and the dinosaur is named after the place where its fossils were discovered – Mamen Stream.

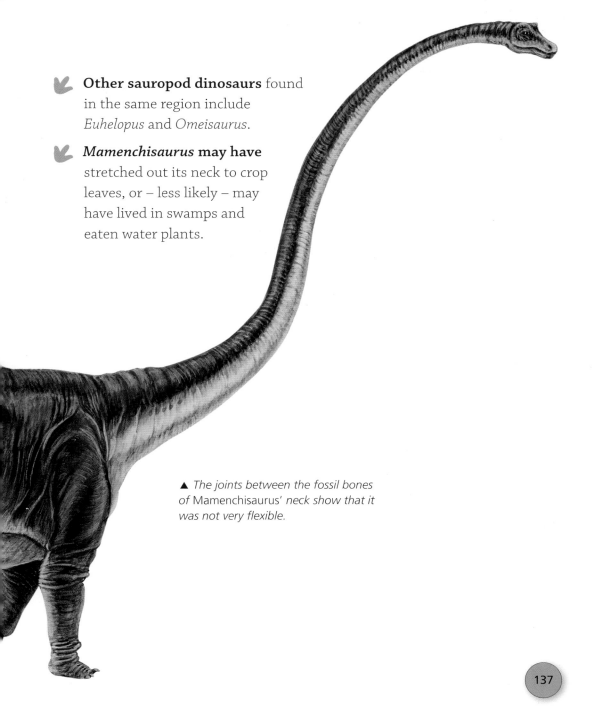

- **Other sauropod dinosaurs** found in the same region include *Euhelopus* and *Omeisaurus*.

- ***Mamenchisaurus* may have** stretched out its neck to crop leaves, or – less likely – may have lived in swamps and eaten water plants.

▲ *The joints between the fossil bones of* Mamenchisaurus' *neck show that it was not very flexible.*

Segnosaurs

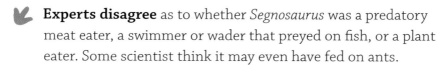

- **Little is known** about the segnosaur group of dinosaurs – it is the subject of much disagreement among experts.

- **Segnosaurs are named** after almost the only known member of the group, *Segnosaurus*.

- **The name *Segnosaurus*** means 'slow reptile'. It lived during the Mid to Late Cretaceous Period, about 90 mya.

- **Fossils of *Segnosaurus*** were found mainly in the Gobi Desert in Central Asia in the 1970s. The dinosaur was named in 1979 by Mongolian scientist Altangerel Perle.

- ***Segnosaurus* had** a narrow head and probably a toothless, beaklike front to its mouth.

- **Experts disagree** as to whether *Segnosaurus* was a predatory meat eater, a swimmer or wader that preyed on fish, or a plant eater. Some scientist think it may even have fed on ants.

- ***Segnosaurus* is now** usually included in the group called therizinosaurs or 'scythe lizards'.

Some scientists have suggested that *Segnosaurus* was a 6-m-long dinosaur version of today's anteater, which rips open termite and ant nests with powerful claws.

▼ Segnosaurus *remains a mystery – even its diet is hotly debated by experts.*

DID YOU KNOW?
Segnosaurus was a sizeable dinosaur, probably about 6.5 m long and standing 3 m tall.

Scelidosaurus

🐾 *Scelidosaurus* **was** a medium-sized armoured dinosaur, perhaps an early member of the ankylosaur group.

🐾 **Fossils of *Scelidosaurus*** have been found in North America, Europe and possibly Asia. It lived during the Early Jurassic Period, about 200 mya.

🐾 **From nose to tail**, *Scelidosaurus* was about 4 m long.

🐾 *Scelidosaurus* **probably** moved about on four legs, although it could perhaps rear up to gather food.

▶ Scelidosaurus *was a widespread dinosaur and a forerunner of bigger, more heavily armoured dinosaur types.*

- **A plant eater**, *Scelidosaurus* snipped off its food with the beaklike front of its mouth, and chewed it with its simple, leaf-shaped teeth.

- *Scelidosaurus* **is one** of the earliest dinosaurs known to have had a set of protective, bony armour plates.

- **A row of bony plates**, or scutes, stuck up from *Scelidosaurus'* neck, back and tail. It also had rows of conical bony plates along its flanks, resembling limpets on a rock.

- *Scelidosaurus* **was described** in 1859, and named in 1863, by Richard Owen, who also invented the name 'dinosaur'.

Stegosaurs

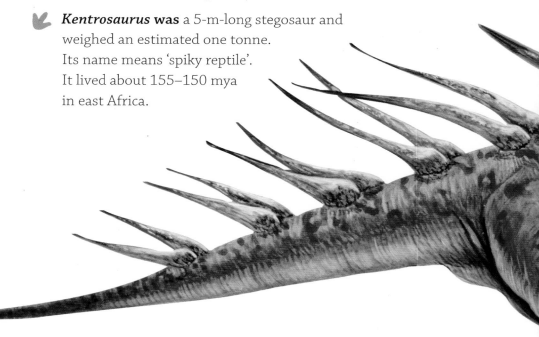

- **Plant-eating dinosaurs** that mostly lived around 160–140 mya, stegosaurs are named after the best known of their group, *Stegosaurus*.

- **They are often called** 'plated dinosaurs', from the large, flat plates or slabs of bone on their backs.

- **Stegosaurs probably** first appeared in eastern Asia, then spread to other continents, especially North America and Africa.

- ***Kentrosaurus was*** a 5-m-long stegosaur and weighed an estimated one tonne. Its name means 'spiky reptile'. It lived about 155–150 mya in east Africa.

▶ *The back plates of Kentrosaurus were taller and narrower than those of* Stegosaurus.

Most stegosaurs lacked teeth at the front of the mouth, but had horny beaks, like those of birds, for snipping off leaves. They chewed food with small, ridged cheek teeth.

DID YOU KNOW?

In 2006, fossils of Stegosaurus were identified in Portugal, which is the first evidence that this dinosaur lived in Europe.

143

Stegosaurus

Stegosaurus **was the largest** of the stegosaur group. Its fossils were found mainly in present-day Colorado, Utah and Wyoming, USA.

Like most of its group, *Stegosaurus* lived towards the end of the Jurassic Period, about 150 mya.

Stegosaurus **was about 8–9 m** long from nose to tail and probably weighed more than 2 tonnes.

Its most striking feature was the large, roughly triangular bony plates along its back.

The name *Stegosaurus* means 'roof reptile'. This is because it was first thought that its bony plates lay flat on its back, overlapping like the tiles on a roof.

 **It is now thought** that the back plates stood upright in two long rows.

 **The plates** may have been for body temperature control, allowing the dinosaur to warm up quickly if it stood side-on to the sun's rays.

 **The back plates** may have been covered with brightly coloured skin, possibly to intimidate enemies – they were too flimsy for protection.

 **Armed with four large** spikes, *Stegosaurus* probably used its tail for swinging at enemies in self defence.

◀ Stegosaurus' *short front limbs meant that it ate low-growing plants.*

145

Tuojiangosaurus

Tuojiangosaurus **was** part of the stegosaur group. It lived during the Late Jurassic Period, about 155 mya.

The first nearly complete dinosaur skeleton to be found in China was of a *Tuojiangosaurus*, and fossil skeletons are on display in several Chinese museums.

The name *Tuojiangosaurus* means 'Tuo River reptile'.

Tuojiangosaurus **was** 7 m long from nose to tail and probably weighed about one tonne.

▶ Tuojiangosaurus *had four long V-shaped spikes on its tail that it swung at enemies in self defence.*

 **Like other stegosaurs,** *Tuojiangosaurus* had tall plates of bone on its back.

 **The back plates** were roughly triangular and probably stood upright in two rows that ran from the neck to the middle of the tail.

 ***Tuojiangosaurus*** **plucked** low-growing plants with its beak-shaped mouth, and partly chewed them with its ridged cheek teeth.

Ankylosaurs

- **Ankylosaurs had** a protective armour of bony plates.

- **Unlike the armoured nodosaurs**, ankylosaurs had a large lump of bone at the end of their tail, which they used as a hammer or club.

- **One of the best known ankylosaurs**, from the preserved remains of about 40 individuals, is *Euoplocephalus*.

- **The hefty *Euoplocephalus*** was about 7 m long and weighed 2 tonnes or more. It lived about 75–70 mya in Alberta, Canada and Montana, USA.

◀ The tail club was made from pieces of bone that had fused (stuck) together.

148

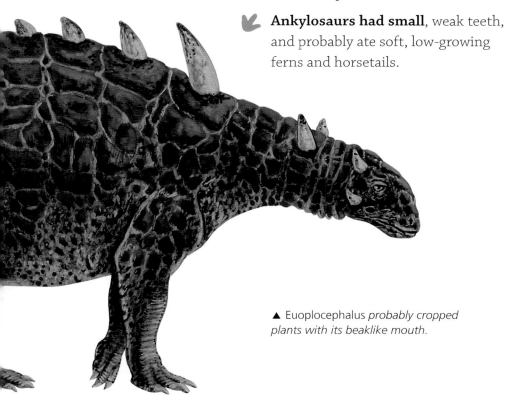

- *Euoplocephalus* **had bony shields** on its head and body, and even had bony eyelids. Blunt spikes ran along its back.

- **Specimens of *Euoplocephalus*** are usually found singly, so it proba[bly] did not live in herds.

- **The ankylosaur *Pinacosaurus*** had bony nodules like chainmail armour in its skin, and rows of blunt spikes from neck to tail.

- **Ankylosaurs had small**, weak teeth, and probably ate soft, low-growing ferns and horsetails.

▲ Euoplocephalus *probably cropped plants with its beaklike mouth.*

149

Nodosaurs

- **Nodosaurs were a subgroup** of armoured dinosaurs in the main ankylosaur group.

- **The nodosaur subgroup** included *Edmontonia*, *Sauropelta*, *Polacanthus* and *Nodosaurus*.

- **Nodosaurs were slow-moving**, heavy-bodied plant eaters with thick, heavy nodules, lumps and plates of bone in their skin for protection.

- **Most nodosaurs lived** during the Late Jurassic and Cretaceous Periods, 150–65 mya.

- *Edmontonia* **lived** in North America during the Late Cretaceous Period, 75–70 mya.

- **It was about 7 m** long, but its bony armour made it very heavy for its size, at 4–5 tonnes.

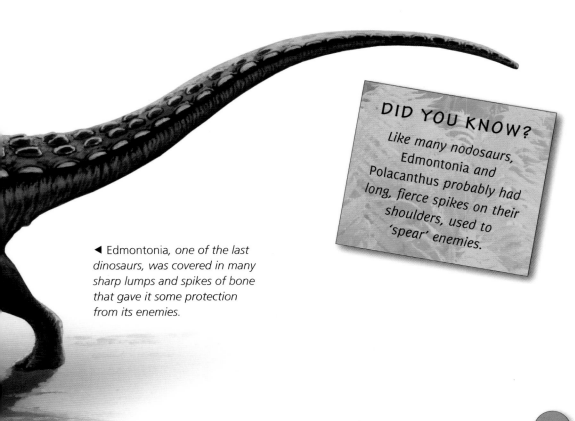

- **Along its neck**, back and tail *Edmontonia* had rows of flat and spiky plates.

- **The nodosaur *Polacanthus*** was about 4 m long and lived 120–110 mya.

- **Fossils of *Polacanthus*** come from the Isle of Wight, England, and perhaps from North America, in South Dakota, USA.

DID YOU KNOW?
Like many nodosaurs, Edmontonia and Polacanthus probably had long, fierce spikes on their shoulders, used to 'spear' enemies.

◄ Edmontonia, *one of the last dinosaurs, was covered in many sharp lumps and spikes of bone that gave it some protection from its enemies.*

Sauropelta

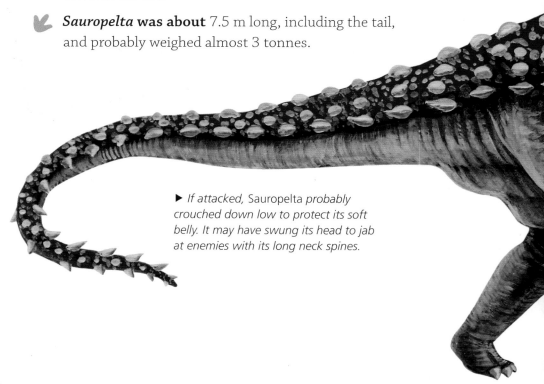

- *Sauropelta* **was a nodosaur** – a type of armoured dinosaur.

- **The name** *Sauropelta* means 'shielded reptile', from the many large, cone-like lumps of bone – some almost as big as dinner plates – on its head, neck, back and tail.

- **The larger lumps of bone** on *Sauropelta* were interspersed with smaller, fist-sized bony studs.

- *Sauropelta* **had a row** of sharp spikes along each side of its body, from just behind the eyes to the tail. The spikes decreased in size towards the tail.

- *Sauropelta* **was about** 7.5 m long, including the tail, and probably weighed almost 3 tonnes.

▶ If attacked, Sauropelta *probably crouched down low to protect its soft belly. It may have swung its head to jab at enemies with its long neck spines.*

The armour of *Sauropelta* was flexible, almost like lumps of metal set into thick leather, so the dinosaur could twist and turn, but was unable to run fast.

Pillar-like legs supported *Sauropelta's* weight.

Using its beaklike mouth, *Sauropelta* probably plucked its low-growing plant food.

DID YOU KNOW?

Sauropelta lived 110–100 mya, in present-day Montana and Wyoming, USA.

Estimating size

- **The biggest dinosaurs** were the sauropods such as *Brachiosaurus* and *Argentinosaurus* – but working out how heavy they were when they were alive is very difficult.

- *Brachiosaurus* **is known** from many remains, including almost complete skeletons, so its length can be measured accurately.

- **A dinosaur's weight** can be estimated from a model of its skeleton, which is 'fleshed out' with clay.

- **The clay represents** muscles, guts and skin, which are based on those of similar reptiles, such as crocodiles, for comparison. Increasingly, this is done using a virtual model on a computer with a 3D skeleton that uses a memory database.

Huge, heavy tail to swing at attackers

Long neck allowed head to browse widely

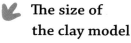 **The size of the clay model** is estimated by immersing it in water to find its volume.

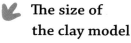 **The volume of the model** is scaled up to find the volume of the real dinosaur when it was alive.

▲ *It is thought that despite its massive size,* Apatosaurus *would have been able to trot surprisingly quickly on its relatively long legs.*

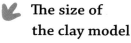 **The sauropod *Apatosaurus*** is now well known from about 12 skeletons, which between them have almost every bone in its body.

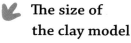 **Experts have 'fleshed out'** the skeleton of *Apatosaurus* by different amounts, so estimates of its weight vary from 20 tonnes to more than 50 tonnes.

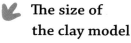 **The length of *Apatosaurus*** is known accurately to have been 21 m in total.

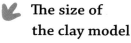 **Fossils of *Brontosaurus*** were found to be identical to those of *Apatosaurus*, and since the name *Apatosaurus* had been given first, this was the name that had to be kept – so, officially, there is no dinosaur called *Brontosaurus*.

◄ *Reconstruction of* Argentinosaurus *is based on relatively few of its own bones, combined with other bones from similar sauropod dinosaurs.*

DID YOU KNOW?

The weights and volumes of reptiles alive today are used to calculate the probable weight of a dinosaur when it was alive.

155

Fabrosaurs

🦶 **Fabrosaurs were small** dinosaurs that lived towards the beginning of the Jurassic Period, about 208–200 mya.

🦶 **The group was named** from *Fabrosaurus*, a dinosaur that was itself named in 1964 from the fossil of a piece of lower jaw bone found in southern Africa.

▲ *On the outside,* Lesothosaurus *looked similar to small predatory dinosaurs such as* Compsognathus. *But its fossil teeth and jaws show that it was probably a plant eater and an early member of the ornithischian group.*

- ***Lesothosaurus* was a fabrosaur,** the fossils of which were found in the Lesotho region of Africa, near the *Fabrosaurus* fossil. It was named in 1978.

- **The lightly built** *Lesothosaurus* was only one metre long from nose to tail-tip and would have stood knee-high to an adult human.

- **Long, slim back legs** and long toes indicate that *Lesothosaurus* was a fast runner.

- **The teeth and other fossils** of *Lesothosaurus* show that it probably ate low-growing plants such as ferns.

- ***Lesothosaurus's* teeth** were set inwards slightly from the sides of its skull, suggesting it had fleshy cheek pouches for storing or chewing food.

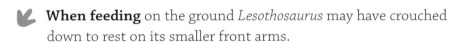

- **When feeding** on the ground *Lesothosaurus* may have crouched down to rest on its smaller front arms.

- ***Lesothosaurus* probably lived in herds**, grazing and browsing, and then racing away at speed from danger.

- **Some experts believe** that *Lesothosaurus* and *Fabrosaurus* were the same, and that the two sets of fossils were wrongly given different names.

157

Heterodontosaurus

- *Heterodontosaurus* **lived** about 205–195 mya, at the beginning of the Jurassic Period.

- **A very small dinosaur** at only 1.2 m in length (about as long as a large dog), *Heterodontosaurus* would have stood knee-high to a human.

- **Probably standing partly upright** on its longer back legs, *Heterodontosaurus* would have been a fast runner.

- **Fossils of *Heterodontosaurus*** come from Lesotho in southern Africa and Cape Province in South Africa.

▼ Heterodontosaurus *probably ate low-growing plants such as ferns.*

- **Most dinosaurs had teeth** of only one shape in their jaws, but *Heterodontosaurus* had three types of teeth.

- **The front teeth** were small, sharp and found only in the upper jaw. They bit against the horny, beaklike lower front of the mouth.

- **The four middle teeth** of *Heterodontosaurus* were long and curved, similar to the tusks of a wild boar, and were perhaps used for fighting rivals or in self defence.

- **The back teeth** were long and had sharp tops, or cusps, for chewing.

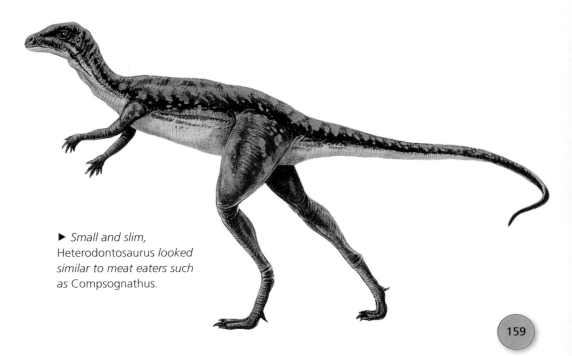

▶ *Small and slim,* Heterodontosaurus *looked similar to meat eaters such as* Compsognathus.

159

Iguanodon

- **Part of the ornithopod group**, *Iguanodon* was a large plant-eating dinosaur. It lived during the Early to Middle Cretaceous Period, 140–110 mya.

- **Numerous fossils** of *Iguanodon* have been found in several countries in Europe, including England, Belgium, Germany and Spain.

- *Iguanodon* **measured** about 9 m from nose to tail. It probably weighed about the same as a large elephant – 4–5 tonnes.

- *Iguanodon* **probably walked** and ran on its large, powerful back legs for much of the time, with its body held horizontal.

- **A cone-shaped spike** on the thumb may have been used as a weapon for jabbing at rivals or enemies.

DID YOU KNOW?
Iguanodon was one of the very first dinosaurs to be given an official scientific name, in 1825.

- **The three central fingers** on the hands had hooflike claws for occasional four-legged walking.

- **The fifth or little finger** was able to bend across the hand for grasping objects, and was perhaps used to pull plants towards the mouth.

▼ Iguanodon *is well known from the fossils of many individuals.*

Thumb spike

▲ *The thumb spike was used in defence and the fingers grasped food.*

Duckbills

- **The common name** for the hadrosaur group of dinosaurs is 'duckbills'.

- **Hadrosaurs were big plant eaters** that walked mainly on their two large, powerful rear legs. They were one of the last main dinosaur groups to appear on Earth, less than 100 mya.

- **Hadrosaurs were named** after *Hadrosaurus*, the first dinosaur of the group to be discovered as fossils, found in 1858 in New Jersey, USA.

- **Most hadrosaurs** had wide mouths that were flattened and toothless at the front, like a duck's beak.

- **Huge numbers of cheek teeth** filled the back of the hadrosaur's mouth, arranged in rows called batteries. They were ideal for chewing tough plant food.

- **Some hadrosaurs** had tall, elaborate crests or projections of bone on their heads, notably *Corythosaurus*, *Saurolophus* and *Parasaurolophus*.

- **Hadrosaurs that lacked** bony crests and had low, smooth heads included *Anatosaurus*, *Bactrosaurus*, *Kritosaurus* and *Edmontosaurus*.

- **The name *Hadrosaurus*** means 'big reptile'.

DID YOU KNOW?

Edmontosaurus may have had a loose bag of skin on its nose that it blew up like a balloon to make a honking or trumpeting noise – perhaps a breeding call.

▼ *Hadrosaurs such as* Parasaurolophus *are often shown feeding on water plants with their wide, ducklike beaked mouths.*

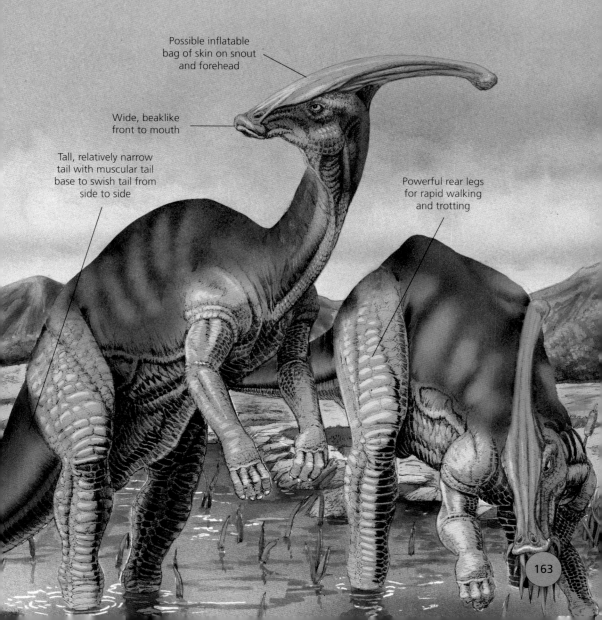

Possible inflatable bag of skin on snout and forehead

Wide, beaklike front to mouth

Tall, relatively narrow tail with muscular tail base to swish tail from side to side

Powerful rear legs for rapid walking and trotting

Psittacosaurus

- ***Psittacosaurus* was** a plant eater in the group known as ceratopsians, or 'horn-faced' dinosaurs.

- **Appearing in the Middle Cretaceous Period**, *Psittacosaurus* lived about 115–110 mya.

▼ *In one fossil discovery, an adult* Psittacosaurus *was found with more than 30 young, which it may have been looking after.*

- *Psittacosaurus* **was named** in 1923 from fossils found in Mongolia, Central Asia. Fossils have been found at various sites across Asia, including Russia, China and Thailand.

- **The rear legs** of *Psittacosaurus* were longer and stronger than its front legs, suggesting that this dinosaur may have reared up to run fast on its rear legs, rather than running on all four legs.

- *Psittacosaurus* **measured** about 2 m long and had four toes on each foot.

- **The name** *Psittacosaurus* means 'parrot reptile', after the dinosaur's beak-shaped mouth, like that of a parrot.

- **Inside its cheeks**, *Psittacosaurus* had many sharp teeth capable of cutting and slicing through tough plant material.

DID YOU KNOW?

Fossil evidence shows that when newly hatched from their eggs, baby Psittacosaurus were hardly longer than a human hand.

Ceratopsians

🐾 **Ceratopsians were** large plant eaters that appeared less than 90 mya.

🐾 **Most ceratopsian fossils** come from North America.

🐾 **Ceratopsian means 'horn-face'**, after the long horns on the dinosaurs' snouts, eyebrows or foreheads.

🐾 **Most ceratopsians** had a neck shield or frill that swept sideways and up from the back of the head to cover the upper neck and shoulders.

🐾 **Well known ceratopsians** include *Triceratops*, *Styracosaurus*, *Centrosaurus*, *Pentaceratops*, *Anchiceratops*, *Chasmosaurus* and *Torosaurus*.

🐾 **The neck frills** of some ceratopsians, such as that of *Chasmosaurus*, had large gaps or 'windows' in the bone.

🐾 **The windows in the neck frill** were covered with thick, scaly skin.

🐾 **Ceratopsians** had no teeth in the fronts of their hooked, beaklike mouths.

🐾 **Using rows** of powerful cheek teeth, ceratopsians sheared off their plant food.

DID YOU KNOW?
Torosaurus had one of the longest skulls of any land animal ever, at about 2.5 m from the front of the snout to the rear of the neck frill.

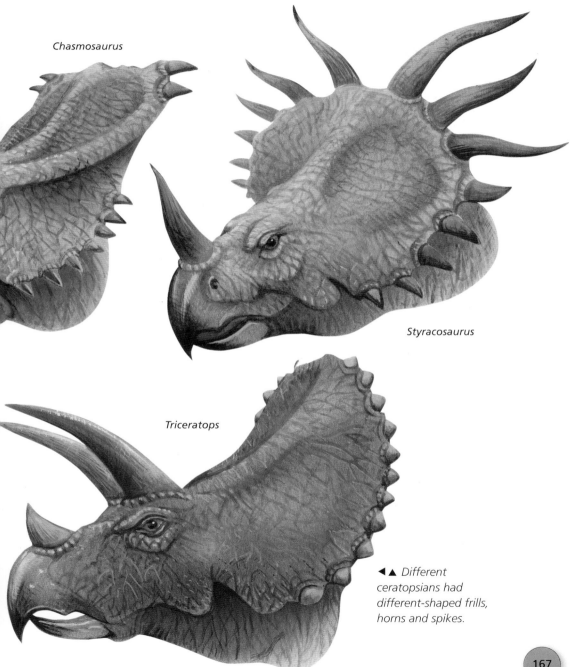

Chasmosaurus

Styracosaurus

Triceratops

◀▲ *Different ceratopsians had different-shaped frills, horns and spikes.*

Triceratops

🐾 **Many fossil remains** of *Triceratops* have been found. It is one of the most-studied and best known dinosaurs and lived at the very end of the Age of Dinosaurs, 67–65 mya.

🐾 *Triceratops* **was the largest** of the plant-eating ceratopsians, or 'horn-faced' dinosaurs.

🐾 **Fossils of about 50** *Triceratops* have been found in North America, though no complete skeleton has been discovered.

🐾 *Triceratops* **was about 9 m** long and weighed about 5–6 tonnes – as big as the largest elephants of today.

🐾 **As well as a short nose horn** and two one-metre eyebrow horns, *Triceratops* also had a wide, sweeping frill that covered its neck like a curved plate.

🐾 **The neck frill** may have been an anchor for the dinosaur's powerful chewing muscles.

🐾 **Acting as a shield**, the bony neck frill may have protected *Triceratops* as it faced predators head-on.

🐾 **The neck frill** may also have been brightly coloured to impress rivals or enemies – or even potential mates.

🐾 **The beaklike front** of *Triceratops*' mouth was toothless, but it had sharp teeth for chewing in its cheeks.

▶ *The beak, head and neck frill of* Triceratops *made up almost a quarter of its length.*

Pachycephalosaurs

🦶 **Pachycephalosaurs were** one of the last dinosaur groups to appear. They lived 75–65 mya.

🦶 **They are named** after one of the best known members of the group, *Pachycephalosaurus*.

🦶 *Pachycephalosaurus* means 'thick-headed reptile', due to the domed and hugely thickened bone on the top of its skull – like a cyclist's crash helmet.

🦶 **About 4.5 m long** from nose to tail, *Pachycephalosaurus* lived in the American Midwest.

▶ *Typical of its group,* Pachycephalosaurus *had a thickened layer of bone on the top of its head.*

Extra thick
skull bone

▲ Wannanosaurus
*was one of the smallest
pachycephalosaurs, at just
one metre long. Some scientists suggest it had
head-butting contests with rivals, but others say
the head dome was used mainly for defence.*

Stegoceras, also from the American Midwest, was
about 2.5 m long with a body the size of a goat.

Homalocephale was about 3 m long and had a flatter skull. It
lived in east Asia.

Pachycephalosaurs may have defended themselves by lowering
their heads and charging at their enemies.

At breeding time, the males may have engaged in head-butting
contests, as some sheep and goats do today.

171

Skin

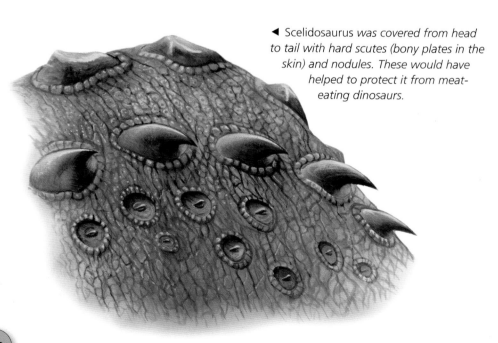 **Several fossils of dinosaur skin** have been found, revealing that dinosaurs had scales like today's reptiles.

As in crocodiles, dinosaur scales were embedded in the thick, tough hide, rather than lying on top of the skin and overlapping, as in snakes.

When the first fossils of dinosaur skin were found in the mid 1800s, scientists thought they were from giant prehistoric crocodiles.

Fossil skin of the horned dinosaur *Chasmosaurus* reveals that larger bumps or lumps, called tubercles, were scattered among the normal-sized scales.

◀ Scelidosaurus *was covered from head to tail with hard scutes (bony plates in the skin) and nodules. These would have helped to protect it from meat-eating dinosaurs.*

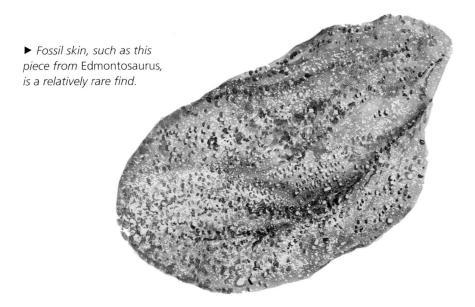

► *Fossil skin, such as this piece from* Edmontosaurus, *is a relatively rare find.*

- **Fossil skin** of the duckbilled hadrosaur *Edmontosaurus* has also been found.

- ***Edmontosaurus* was covered** in thousands of small scales, like little pebbles, with larger lumps or tubercles spaced among them.

- **Various specimens** of fossil skin show that the scales of *Iguanodon*-type dinosaurs were larger than those of same-sized, similar duckbill dinosaurs.

- **Scaly skin** protected a dinosaur against the teeth and claws of enemies, accidental scrapes, and the bites of pests such as mosquitoes and fleas.

DID YOU KNOW?
Many dinosaur scales were roughly six-sided, which made them both strong and flexible.

173

Colours

- **No one knows** for certain what colours dinosaurs were.

- **Some fossil specimens** of dinosaur skin show patterns or shading, but all are stone coloured, as fossils are living things that have turned to stone.

- **Some experts believe** that dinosaurs were similar in colour to crocodiles – dull greens and browns.

- **Dinosaurs that were** dull greens and browns would have been well camouflaged among trees, rocks and earth.

- **According to some experts**, certain dinosaurs may have been bright yellow, red or blue, and possibly striped or patched, like some of today's lizards and snakes.

- **Some dinosaurs** may have been brightly coloured to frighten off predators or to intimidate rivals at breeding time. Colours may have also attracted potential mates.

- **Tall 'sails'** on the backs of the plant eater *Ouranosaurus* and the meat eater *Spinosaurus* may have been for visual display, as well as for temperature control.

- **The large, bony back plates** on stegosaurs may have been used for colourful displays to rivals and mates.

- **The large neck frills** of dinosaurs such as *Triceratops* may have been colourful and used for display.

Recent finds of dinosaur skin reveal microscopic ridges and patterns on the scales. These may have reflected light to give an appearance of colour.

▲ Dilong *had hairlike feathers, However, like all reconstructions from fossils, the colours are intelligent guesswork.*

175

Armour

- **Many kinds of dinosaurs** had protective 'armour'.

- **Some armour** took the form of bony plates, or osteoderms, embedded in the skin.

- **A dinosaur with armour** might weigh twice as much as a same-sized dinosaur without armour.

- **Armoured dinosaurs** are divided into two main groups – the ankylosaurs and the nodosaurs.

- **The large sauropod** *Saltasaurus* had a kind of armour in the form of hundreds of small, bony lumps, each as big as a pea, packed together in the skin of its back.

- **On its back**, *Saltasaurus* also had about 50 larger pieces of bone, each one the size of a human hand.

- ***Saltasaurus* is named** after the Salta region of Argentina, where its fossils were found. Its fossils have also been found in Uruguay, South America.

- ***Saltasaurus* was 12 m** long and weighed about 6–8 tonnes.

◀ Ankylosaurus swings its tail as a defensive weapon against a spinosaur. The tail club was nearly one metre across.

177

Horns

- **A dinosaur's horns got bigger** as the animal grew. Each horn had a bony core and an outer covering of a tough material formed mainly from keratin – the same substance that makes up human hair and fingernails.

- **Horns were most common** among plant-eating dinosaurs. They were probably used for defence and to protect young against predators.

- **The biggest horns** belonged to the ceratopsians or 'horn-faces', such as *Triceratops*.

- **In some ceratopsian horns**, the bony core alone was about one metre long. This did not include the outer sheath, so the whole horn would have been longer.

- **The ceratopsian *Styracosaurus***, or 'spiked reptile', had a series of long horns around the top of its neck frill, and a very long horn on its nose.

DID YOU KNOW?

Dinosaurs may have used their horns to push over plants or dig up roots for food.

Horns may have been used in head-swinging displays to intimidate rivals and make physical fighting less likely.

In battle, male dinosaurs may have locked horns in a trial of strength, as antelopes do today.

Armoured dinosaurs such as the nodosaur *Panoplosaurus* had hornlike spikes along the sides of the body, especially in the shoulder region.

▼ *If an enemy came near* Triceratops *charged with its head down, and jabbed with its long, sharp horns. The wide frill of bone over its neck made it look even more scary.*

179

Head crests

- **Many dinosaurs** had lumps, plates, ridges or other shapes of bone on their heads, called head crests.

- **Head crests** may have been covered with brightly coloured skin for visual display.

- **Meat eaters with head crests** included *Carnotaurus* and *Dilophosaurus*.

- **The dinosaurs with the largest** and most complicated head crests were the hadrosaurs.

- **The largest head crest** was probably a long, hollow, tubular shape of bone belonging to the hadrosaur *Parasaurolophus*.

- **The head crests** of hadrosaurs may have been involved in making sounds.

DID YOU KNOW?
The head crests of some large Parasaurolophus, perhaps full-grown males, reached an incredible 1.8 m in length.

Some years ago, the hadrosaur *Tsintaosaurus* was thought to have a very unusual head crest – a hollow tube sticking straight up between the eyes, like a unicorn's horn.

The so-called head crest of *Tsintaosaurus* is now thought to be the fossil part of another animal, and not part of *Tsintaosaurus* at all.

***Tsintaosaurus* is now** usually known as *Tanius*, a hadrosaur with a small crest or no crest at all!

▼ *The long crest of* Parasaurolophus *may have had a flap of skin behind it.*

181

Teeth

- **Some of the most common** fossil remains are of dinosaur teeth – the hardest parts of their bodies.

- **Dinosaur teeth** come in a huge range of sizes and shapes – daggers, knives, shears, pegs, combs, rakes, file-like rasps, crushing batteries and vices.

- **In some dinosaurs**, up to three-quarters of a tooth was fixed into the jaw bone, so only one-quarter showed.

- **The teeth of plant eaters** such as *Iguanodon* had angled tops that rubbed past each other in a grinding motion.

- **Some duckbill dinosaurs** (hadrosaurs) had more than 1000 teeth, all at the back of the mouth.

▼ ▶ *The shape, number and layout of teeth indicated what food a dinosaur ate.*

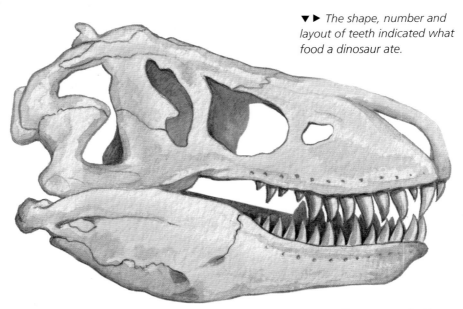

Tyrannosaurus had long, sharp teeth for tearing flesh and crushing bone

🦅 **Like modern reptiles**, dinosaurs probably grew new teeth to replace old, worn or broken ones.

🦅 **Some of the largest teeth** of any dinosaur belonged to 9-m-long *Daspletosaurus*, a tyrannosaur-like meat eater. They measured up to 18 cm in length.

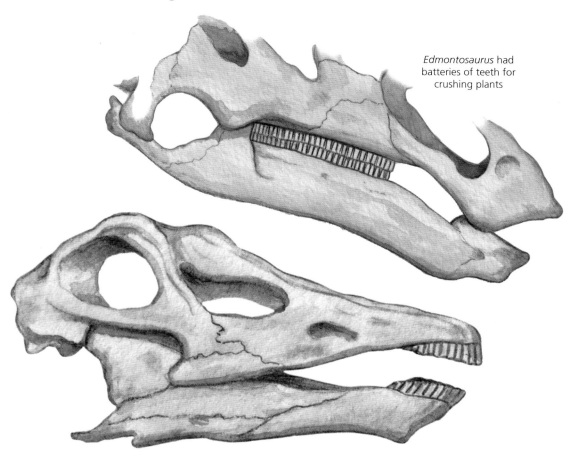

Edmontosaurus had batteries of teeth for crushing plants

Apatosaurus had peglike teeth for raking leaves from branches

183

Beaks

- **Several kinds of dinosaurs** had a toothless, beak-shaped front to their mouths.

- **Beaked dinosaurs** included ceratopsians (horn-faces) such as *Triceratops*, ornithopods such as *Iguanodon* and the hadrosaurs (duckbills), stegosaurs, segnosaurs, ankylosaurs (armoured dinosaurs) and fast-running ostrich dinosaurs.

▶ Psittacosaurus *seemed to be an early member of the dinosaur group known as the ceratopsians or horn-faces. It had the characteristic birdlike beak, but had not yet evolved the face horns or neck shield.*

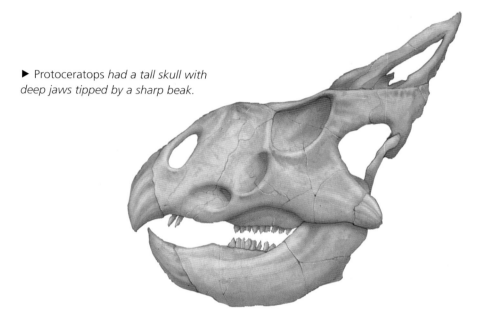

▶ Protoceratops *had a tall skull with deep jaws tipped by a sharp beak.*

🐾 **Most beaked dinosaurs** had chopping or chewing teeth near the backs of their mouths, in their cheeks, but ostrich dinosaurs had no teeth.

🐾 **A dinosaur's beak** was made up of the upper (maxilla) and the lower (dentary or mandible) jaw bones.

🐾 **The bones at the front** of a dinosaur's jaw would have been covered with horn, which formed the outer shape of the beak.

🐾 **Dinosaurs almost certainly** used their beaks for pecking, snipping, tearing and slicing their food. They may also have used their beaks to peck fiercely at any attackers.

DID YOU KNOW?

Some of the largest beaks in relation to body size belonged to Oviraptor and Psittacosaurus.

Noses

🦶 **Dinosaurs breathed** through their mouths and/or noses, like many other creatures today.

🦶 **Fossil dinosaur skulls** show that there were two nose openings, called nares, in the bone.

🦶 **The nasal openings**, or nares, led to nasal chambers inside the skull, where the smell organs were located.

🦶 **Some meat eaters**, especially carnosaurs such as *Allosaurus* and *Tyrannosaurus*, had very large nasal chambers and probably had an excellent sense of smell.

🦶 **In most dinosaurs**, the nasal openings were at the front of the snout, just above the upper jaw.

🦶 **In some dinosaurs**, especially sauropods such as *Mamenchisaurus* and *Brachiosaurus*, the nasal openings were higher on the skull, between the eyes.

🦶 **Fossils show that** air passages led backwards from the nasal chambers into the head for breathing.

DID YOU KNOW?
In hadrosaurs, the nasal passages inside the bony head crests were more than one metre long.

The nasal openings led to external openings, or nostrils, in the skin.

New evidence from modern animals suggests that a dinosaur's nostrils would have been lower down than the nares, towards the front of the snout.

▼ *The nares (nasal openings) at the snout tip of* Tyrannosaurus *were especially large.*

Nares

Eyes

No fossils have been found of dinosaur eyes because they are made of soft tissue that soon rots away after death, or are eaten by scavengers.

▲ Tyrannosaurus rex *had large eyes that were set at an angle so they looked more to the front rather than to the sides. This allowed* T rex *to see an object in front with both eyes and so judge its distance well.*

▶ *The eye socket of* Troodon *was very large, shown here as the elongated middle opening.*

The main clues to dinosaur eyes come from the hollows, or orbits, in the skull where the eyes were located.

The orbits in fossil skulls show that dinosaur eyes were similar to those of reptiles today.

The 6-m-long sauropod *Vulcanodon* had tiny eyes relative to the size of its head.

Small-eyed dinosaurs probably only had good vision in the daytime.

The eyes of many plant-eating dinosaurs, such as *Vulcanodon*, were on the sides of their heads, giving them all-round vision.

The small meat eater *Troodon* had relatively large eyes, and it could probably see well, even in dim light.

***Troodon's* eyes** were on the front of its face and pointed forwards, allowing it to see detail and judge distance.

Dinosaurs that had large bulges, called optic lobes, in their brains – detectable by the shapes of their skulls – could probably see very well, perhaps even at night.

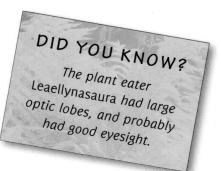

DID YOU KNOW?

The plant eater Leaellynasaura had large optic lobes, and probably had good eyesight.

189

Brains

🦶 **There is a broad link** between the size of an animal's brain compared to the size of its body, and the level of intelligence it shows.

🦶 **Some fossil dinosaur skulls** have preserved the hollow where the brain once was, revealing its approximate size and shape.

🦶 **In some cases**, a lump of rock formed inside a fossil skull, taking on the size and shape of the brain.

🦶 **The tiny brain** of *Stegosaurus* weighed about 70–80 g, while the whole dinosaur weighed up to 2 tonnes.

🦶 **The brain** of *Stegosaurus* was only 1/25,000th of the weight of its whole body (in a human it is 1/50th).

▶ *A peaceful plant eater,* Stegosaurus *would have had little use for the intelligence of a stealthy hunter like* Troodon.

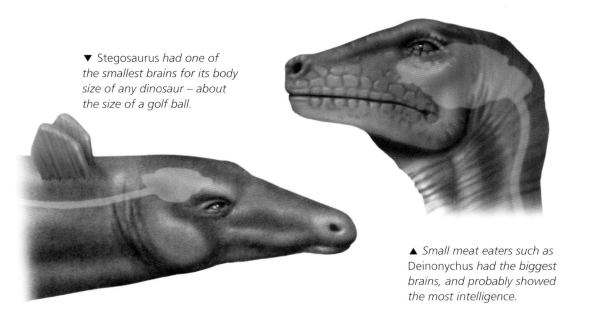

▼ Stegosaurus *had one of the smallest brains for its body size of any dinosaur – about the size of a golf ball.*

▲ *Small meat eaters such as* Deinonychus *had the biggest brains, and probably showed the most intelligence.*

Brachiosaurus' **brain** was perhaps only 1/100,000th of the weight of its whole body.

The brain of the small meat eater *Troodon* was about 1/100th the weight of its body, which means that *Troodon* was probably one of the most intelligent dinosaurs.

The brain-body size comparison for most dinosaurs is much the same as that of living reptiles.

Small- and medium-sized meat eaters such as *Troodon* may have been as 'intelligent' as parrots or rats.

It was once thought that *Stegosaurus* had a 'second brain' in the base of its tail. Now this lump is thought to have been a nerve junction.

191

Stomach stones

- **Some dinosaur fossils** are found with smooth, rounded stones, like seashore pebbles, jumbled up among or near them.

- **Smooth pebbles occur** with dinosaur fossils far more than would be expected by chance alone.

- **These stones** are mainly found with or near the remains of large plant-eating dinosaurs, especially prosauropods such as *Massospondylus*, *Plateosaurus* and *Riojasaurus*, sauropods such as *Brachiosaurus* and *Diplodocus*, the parrot-beaked *Psittacosaurus* and the stegosaurs.

- **Some plant-eating dinosaurs** may have used smooth stones to help process their food.

- **The smooth pebbles** associated with dinosaur remains are known as gastroliths.

- **Gastroliths were stones** that a dinosaur deliberately swallowed.

- **In the stomach**, gastroliths acted as 'millstones', crushing and churning food, and breaking it down into a soft pulp for better digestion.

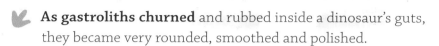

As gastroliths churned and rubbed inside a dinosaur's guts, they became very rounded, smoothed and polished.

Gastroliths may be the reason why many big plant eaters, especially sauropods, had no chewing teeth – the mashing was done inside the guts.

▼ Sauropods, like Barosaurus, did not chew their food before swallowing. Instead, they swallowed stones which ground up the food in a part of the digestive system called the gizzard. This meant that they wasted no time when feeding their huge bodies!

▶ Gastroliths as small as a pea and as large as a football have been found.

Sails

▲ *The predator* Spinosaurus *was almost as large as* Tyrannosaurus. *Its sail would have been almost 2 m tall.*

Long, bony extensions, like rods or spines, stuck up from the backs of some dinosaurs.

These extensions may have held up a large area of skin, commonly called a back sail.

Dinosaurs with back sails included the meat eater *Spinosaurus* and the plant eater *Ouranosaurus*.

Spinosaurus and *Ouranosaurus* both lived over 100 mya.

- Fossils of *Spinosaurus* and *Ouranosaurus* were found in North Africa.

- **The skin on a back sail** may have been brightly coloured, or may even have changed colour, like the skin of a chameleon lizard today.

- **A back sail** may have helped to control body temperature. Standing sideways to the sun, it would absorb the sun's heat and allow the dinosaur to warm up quickly.

- **Standing in the shade**, a back sail would lose warmth and help the dinosaur to avoid overheating.

▼ Apart from its back sail, *Ouranosaurus was similar to its close cousin, the plant eater* Iguanodon.

195

Hips

- **All dinosaurs are classified** in one of two large groups, according to the design and shape of their hip bones.

- **One of these groups** is the Saurischia, meaning 'reptile-hipped'.

- **In a saurischian dinosaur**, the lower front pair of rod-shaped bones in the pelvis project down and forwards.

- **All meat-eating dinosaurs** belonged to the Saurischia.

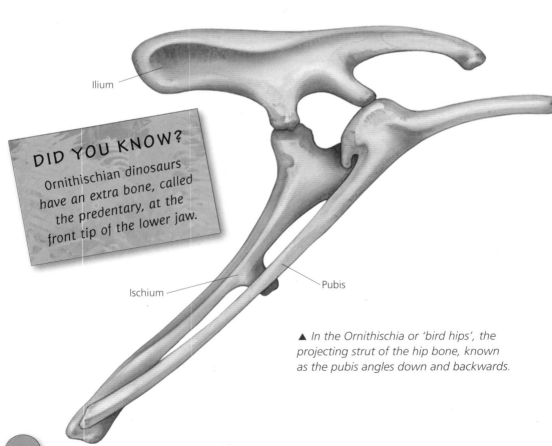

Ilium

DID YOU KNOW?

Ornithischian dinosaurs have an extra bone, called the predentary, at the front tip of the lower jaw.

Ischium

Pubis

▲ In the Ornithischia or 'bird hips', the projecting strut of the hip bone, known as the pubis angles down and backwards.

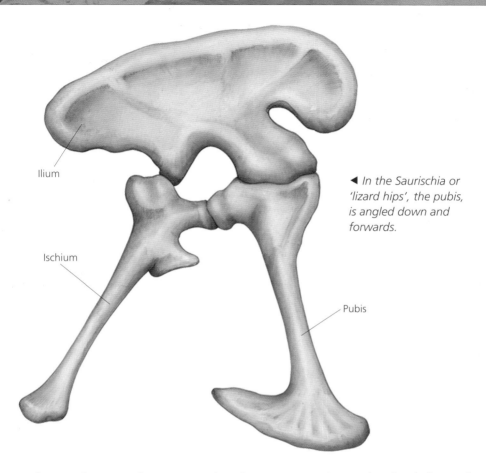

Ilium

Ischium

Pubis

◀ *In the Saurischia or 'lizard hips', the pubis, is angled down and forwards.*

- **The biggest dinosaurs**, the plant-eating sauropods, also belonged to the Saurischia.

- **The second group** is the Ornithischia, meaning 'bird-hipped'.

- **In an ornithischian dinosaur**, the lower front pair of rod-shaped bones in the pelvis, called the pubis bones, project down and backwards, lying parallel with another pair, the ischium bones.

- **All dinosaurs** in the Ornithischia group, from small *Heterodontosaurus* to huge *Triceratops*, were plant eaters.

Legs and posture

- **All dinosaurs had four limbs.** Unlike some other reptiles, such as snakes and slow-worms, they did not lose their limbs through evolution.

- **Some dinosaurs**, such as the massive, plant-eating sauropod *Janenschia*, stood and walked on all four legs nearly all the time.

- **The all-fours method** of standing and walking is called 'quadrupedal'.

- **Some dinosaurs**, such as the nimble, meat-eating dromaeosaur *Deinonychus*, stood and walked on their back limbs only.

- **The back-limbs-only method** of standing and walking is called 'bipedal'.

- **Some dinosaurs**, such as the hadrosaur *Edmontosaurus*, could move on all four limbs or just on their back legs if they chose to.

▲ Cetiosaurus *was a quadrupedal dinosaur with thick, pillar-like legs.*

▶ Tarbosaurus *was a bipedal dinosaur that ran and walked on its back legs. Its strong rear legs contrasted hugely to its puny front arms, which were too small to be used.*

The two- or four-legs method of standing and walking is called 'bipedal/quadrupedal'.

Reptiles such as lizards and crocodiles have a sprawling posture, in which the upper legs join the body at the sides.

Dinosaurs had an upright posture, with the legs directly below the body.

The more efficient upright posture and gait may be one major reason why dinosaurs were so successful compared to other animals of the time.

Feet

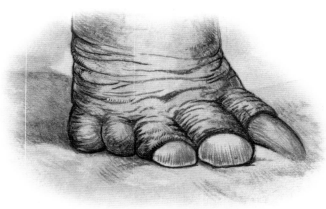

◄ *Each foot of* Apatosaurus *supported more than 5 tonnes.*

- **Dinosaur feet differed**, depending on the animal's body design, weight and lifestyle.

- **A typical dinosaur's front feet** had metacarpal bones in the lower wrist or upper hand, and two or three phalanges bones in each digit (finger or toe), tipped by claws.

- **The rear feet** of a typical dinosaur had metatarsal (instead of metacarpal) bones in the lower ankle.

- **Some dinosaurs** had five toes per foot, like most other reptiles (and most birds and mammals).

- **Sauropods probably had** feet with rounded bases supported by a wedge of fibrous, cushion-like tissue.

- **Most sauropods** had claws on their first three toes, and smaller, blunter 'hooves' on the other two toes.

- **Ostrich dinosaurs** such as *Gallimimus* had very long feet and long, slim toes for running fast.

- **Many fast-running dinosaurs** had fewer toes, to reduce weight – *Gallimimus* had three toes per back foot.

- **The ornithopod**, or 'bird feet' dinosaur group, includes *Iguanodon*, duckbilled dinosaurs, *Heterodontosaurus* and many other plant eaters.

DID YOU KNOW?

The dinosaur group that includes all the meat eaters, both large and small, is named the theropods, or 'beast feet'.

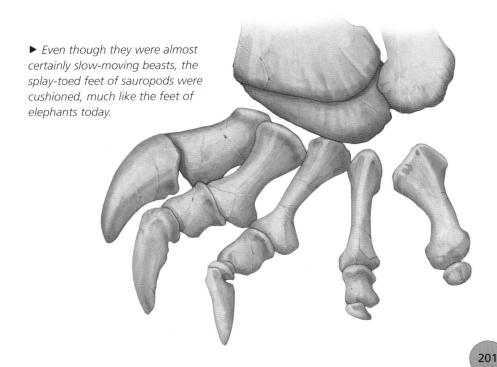

▶ Even though they were almost certainly slow-moving beasts, the splay-toed feet of sauropods were cushioned, much like the feet of elephants today.

Claws

- **Like reptiles today**, dinosaurs had claws or similar hard structures at the ends of their digits (fingers and toes).

- **Dinosaur claws** were probably made from keratin – the same hard substance that formed their horns, and from which our own fingernails and toenails are made.

- **Claw shapes and sizes** relative to body size varied greatly between dinosaurs.

- **In many meat-eating dinosaurs** that ran on two back legs, the claws on the fingers were long and sharp, similar to a cat's claws.

- **A small, meat-eating dinosaur** such as *Troodon* probably used its finger claws for grabbing small mammals and lizards, and for scrabbling in the soil for insects and worms.

- **Larger meat-eating dinosaurs** such as *Allosaurus* may have used their hand claws to hold and slash their prey.

- **Huge plant-eating sauropods** such as *Diplodocus* had claws on its elephant-like feet that resembled nails or hooves.

- **Many dinosaurs** had five-clawed digits on their feet, but some, such as *Tyrannosaurus*, had only three.

Some of the largest claws belonged to *Deinocheirus* – its finger claws were more than 35 cm long.

Deinonychus **had long claws** on its hands and feet that it used to slash at prey. Its name means 'terrible claw' and it lived in the Mid-Cretaceous Period.

▲ *The fingers and claws of* Deinonychus *were especially long and strong.*

203

Tails

- **All dinosaurs** evolved with tails – though some individuals may have lost theirs in attacks or accidents.

- **The length of the tail** relative to the body, and its shape, thickness and special features, gives many clues as to how the dinosaur used it.

- **The longest tails**, at more than 17 m, belonged to the giant plant-eating sauropods such as *Diplodocus*.

- **Some sauropods** had a chain of more than 80 separate bones in the tail – over twice the usual number.

- **Sauropods may have** used their tails as a whip to flick at enemies.

▼ Compsognathus *had a long tail that helped it to balance and turn quickly when it was running fast.*

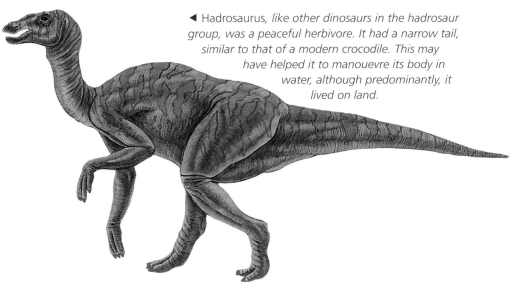

◀ Hadrosaurus, *like other dinosaurs in the hadrosaur group, was a peaceful herbivore. It had a narrow tail, similar to that of a modern crocodile. This may have helped it to manouevre its body in water, although predominantly, it lived on land.*

- **Many meat-eating dinosaurs** that stood or ran on their back legs had thick-based tails to balance the weight of their bodies.

- **Small meat eaters**, such as *Compsognathus*, used their tails for balance when leaping and darting about.

- **The meat eater** *Ornitholestes* had a tail that was more than half of its 2-m length. It was used as a counterbalance and rudder to help it turn corners at speed.

- **Armoured dinosaurs** called ankylosaurs had two huge lumps of bone at the ends of their tails, which they swung at their enemies like a club.

- **The tails of duckbilled dinosaurs** (hadrosaurs) may have been swished from side to side in the water as an aid to swimming.

Male and female

In dinosaur fossils, the shapes of the hip bones and head crests can indicate if the creatures were male or female.

Head crest fossils of different sizes and proportions belonging to the hadrosaur (duckbilled dinosaur) *Lambeosaurus* have been found.

Some *Lambeosaurus* had short, rounded main crests with small, spikelike spurs pointing up and back.

- **Other *Lambeosaurus*** had a large, angular main crest with a large spur pointing up and back.

- **The head crest differences** in *Lambeosaurus* fossils may indicate that males and females looked different.

- **Remains of the hadrosaur** *Corythosaurus* show two main sizes of head crest, perhaps one belonging to females and the other to males.

- **New studies** in the variations of head crests led to more than eight different species of dinosaurs being reclassified as one species of *Corythosaurus*.

DID YOU KNOW?

In Parasaurolophus specimens, some head crests were twice as long as others – probably a male-female difference.

◀ Male and female Lambeosaurus *may have had different-shaped head crests, with this individual being male. The crests may also have become relatively larger compared to body size as the dinosaurs grew.*

Warm or cold blood?

🐾 **If dinosaurs were cold-blooded**, like reptiles today, they would have been slow or inactive in cold conditions.

🐾 **If dinosaurs were warm-blooded**, like birds and mammals today, they would have been able to stay warm and active in cold conditions.

◀ The detailed microscopic structure inside bones can give clues as to warm- or cold-bloodedness.

🐾 **Experts once believed** that all dinosaurs were cold-blooded, but today there is much disagreement.

🐾 **Some evidence** for warm-bloodedness comes from the structure of fossil bones.

🐾 **The structure** of some dinosaur bones is more like that of warm-blooded creatures than of reptiles.

Some small meat eaters may have evolved into birds. As birds are warm-blooded, these dinosaurs may have been, too.

In a 'snapshot' count of dinosaur fossils, the number of predators compared to prey is more like the comparisons seen in mammals than in reptiles.

Some dinosaurs probably lived in herds and raised young, as many birds and mammals do today. In reptiles such behaviour is rare.

If dinosaurs were warm-blooded, they would probably have needed to eat at least ten times more food than if they were cold-blooded, to 'burn' food energy to make heat.

▼ *Crocodiles, which were around even in the very earliest dinosaur period (the Triassic) are cold-blooded.*

209

Speed

- **The fastest dinosaurs** had long, slim, muscular legs and small, lightweight bodies.

- **Ostrich dinosaurs** were probably the speediest, perhaps attaining the same top speed as today's ostrich – 70 km/h.

- **The main leg muscles** of the ostrich dinosaur *Struthiomimus* were in its hips and thighs.

- **The hip and leg design** of ostrich dinosaurs meant they could swing their limbs to and fro quickly, like those of a modern racehorse.

- **Large, powerful, plant-eating dinosaurs**, such as the duckbill *Edmontosaurus*, may have pounded along on their huge back legs at 40 km/h.

- **Plant eaters** such as *Iguanodon* and *Muttaburrasaurus* may have trotted along at 10–12 km/h for many hours.

- **Some experts** once suggested that the great meat eater *Tyrannosaurus* may have been able to run at 50 km/h.

- **Other experts** think *Tyrannosaurus* was a relatively slow runner at 20 km/h.

- **The slowest dinosaurs** were giant sauropods such as *Brachiosaurus*, which probably plodded at 4–6 km/h (about human walking speed).

- **The fastest land animal today**, the cheetah, would beat any dinosaur with its maximum burst of speed of more than 100 km/h.

▼ *In 2007, computer predictions suggested that the top speed of* Tyrannosaurus *was about 28 km/h.*

Coprolites

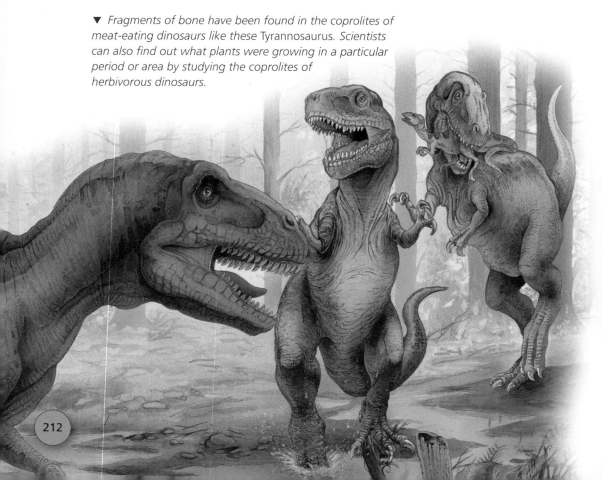

Coprolites are the fossilized droppings, or dung, of animals from long ago, such as dinosaurs. Like other fossils, they have become solid rock.

Thousands of dinosaur coprolites have been found at fossil sites across the world.

Cracking or cutting open coprolites may reveal what the dinosaur had eaten.

▼ *Fragments of bone have been found in the coprolites of meat-eating dinosaurs like these* Tyrannosaurus. *Scientists can also find out what plants were growing in a particular period or area by studying the coprolites of herbivorous dinosaurs.*

- **Coprolites produced** by large meat eaters such as *Tyrannosaurus* contain bone from their prey.

- **The microscopic structure** of the bones found in coprolites shows the age of the prey when it was eaten. Most victims were very young or old, as these were the easiest creatures for a predator to kill.

- **Coprolites produced** by small meat eaters such as *Compsognathus* may contain the hard bits of insects, such as the legs and wing cases of beetles.

- **Huge piles** of coprolites found in Montana, USA, were probably produced by the large plant eater *Maiasaura*.

- *Maiasaura* **coprolites** contain the remains of cones, buds and the needle-like leaves of conifer trees, showing that these dinosaurs had a diet of tough plant matter.

▶ Fossilized dinosaur dung may provide important clues as to the kind of food eaten by dinosaurs.

Footprints

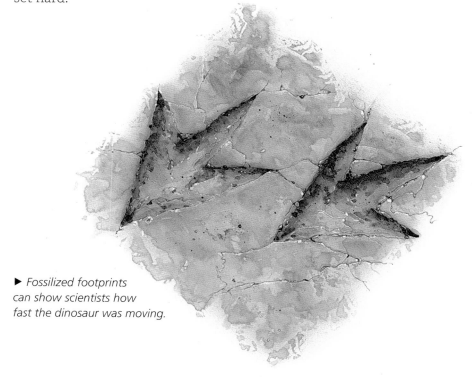

Fossilized dinosaur footprints have been found all over the world.

Some dinosaurs left footprints when they walked on the soft mud or sand of riverbanks. Then the mud baked hard in the sun, and was covered by more sand or mud, which helped preserve the footprints as fossils.

Some footprints were made when dinosaur feet left impressions in soft mud or sand that was then covered by volcanic ash, which set hard.

▶ Fossilized footprints can show scientists how fast the dinosaur was moving.

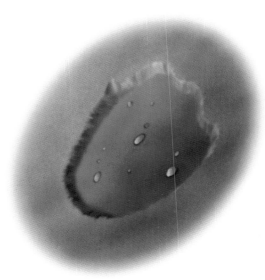

▶ Fossilized footprints are called trace fossils because they are signs or prints made by dinosaurs, or other creatures, rather than actual bodyparts.

Many footprints have been found together in lines, called 'trackways'. These suggest that some dinosaurs lived in groups, or used the same routes regularly.

The distance between same-sized footprints indicates whether a dinosaur was walking, trotting or running.

Footprints of big meat eaters such as *Tyrannosaurus* show three toes with claws, on a forward-facing foot.

In big plant eaters, such as *Iguanodon*, each footprint shows three separate toes, but less or no claw impressions, and the feet point slightly inwards.

In giant plant-eating sauropods, each footprint is rounded and has indentations of nail-like 'hooves'.

Some sauropod footprints are more than one metre across.

DID YOU KNOW?

Eighty-cm-long hadrosaur footprints were found near Salt Lake City, Utah, USA.

215

Herds

🦖 **When fossils** of many individuals of the same dinosaur type are found together, there are various possible causes.

🦖 **One reason** is because their bodies were swept to the same place by a flood.

▼ *A mixed-age herd would have left similar footprints of different sizes.*

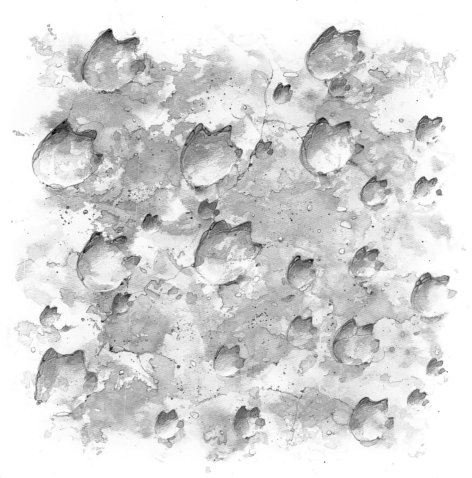

- **The dinosaurs** may have died in the same place if they had lived there as a group or herd.

- **There is much evidence** that various dinosaur types lived in groups or herds, examples being *Diplodocus*, *Triceratops* and *Iguanodon*.

DID YOU KNOW?
At Peace River Canyon, British Columbia, Canada, some 1700 footprints were found.

- **Many fossil footprints** found together suggest that some dinosaurs lived in herds.

- **Some fossil groups** include dinosaurs of different ages, from babies to youngsters and adults.

- **Footprints of** a plant-eating dinosaur have been found with the prints of a meat eater to one side of them – perhaps evidence of a hunter pursuing its victim.

- **Prints all pointing** in the same direction indicate a herd travelling together to the same place.

- **Sometimes larger footprints** are found to the sides of smaller ones, possibly indicating that adults guarded their young between them.

- **Many jumbled prints** in what was once mud suggests a group of dinosaurs came to drink at a riverbank or lakeside.

Migration

- **Today, almost no land** reptiles go on regular, long-distance journeys, called migrations.

- **Over the past 30 years**, some scientists have suggested that certain dinosaurs regularly migrated.

- **Evidence for migrating dinosaurs** comes from the positions of the continents at the time. In certain regions, cool winters would have prevented the growth of enough plants for dinosaurs to eat.

- **Fossil evidence suggests** that some plants stopped growing during very hot or dry times, so some dinosaurs would have migrated to find food.

▼ *Fossils of* Pachyrhinosaurus *have been found in parts of Alaska that were inside the Arctic Circle at the end of the Cretaceous Period. Since they did not live here permanently, it is reasonable to suppose that they migrated here.*

▶ *Few modern reptiles migrate seasonally. Centrosaurus, a dinosaur from the Cretaceous Period, made a migration (indicated here by the arrow) from North America to the sub-Arctic region for the short summer when plant growth was lush.*

- **The footprints or tracks** of many dinosaurs travelling in herds is possible evidence that some dinosaurs migrated.

- **Dinosaurs that may have migrated** include *Centrosaurus* and *Pachyrhinosaurus*, sauropods such as *Diplodocus*, and ornithopods such as *Iguanodon* and *Muttaburrasaurus*.

- **One huge fossil site** in Alberta, Canada, contains the fossils of about 1000 *Pachyrhinosaurus* – perhaps a migrating herd that got caught in a flood.

- **In North America**, huge herds of *Centrosaurus* may have migrated north for the brief sub-Arctic summer, when plants were abundant, providing plentiful food.

- **In autumn**, *Centrosaurus* herds perhaps travelled south again to overwinter in the forests.

Hibernation

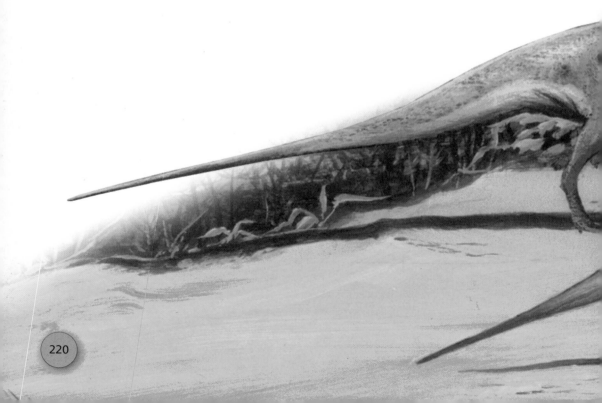

Dinosaurs may have gone into an inactive state called torpor or hibernation during cold periods, as many reptiles do today.

The plant eater *Leaellynasaura*, found at Dinosaur Cove, Australia, may have become torpid due to the yearly cycle of seasons there.

Dinosaur Cove was nearer the South Pole when dinosaurs lived there, 120–100 mya. At this time, the climate was relatively warm, with no ice at the North or South Poles.

Dinosaurs living at Dinosaur Cove would have had to cope with periods of darkness in winter. They may have become torpid to survive the cold.

- **The eye and brain shapes** of *Leaellynasaura* suggest it had good eyesight, which would have helped it to see in the winter darkness, or in dim forests.

- **Dinosaur fossils** have been found in the Arctic region near the North Pole.

- **Arctic dinosaurs** either became torpid in winter, or migrated south to warmer regions.

▼ *Leaellynasaura may have slept through the cold season, perhaps protected in a burrow.*

Sounds

- **Few reptiles today** make complicated sounds, except for simple hisses, grunts, coughs and roars.

- **Fossils suggest** that dinosaurs made a variety of sounds in several different ways.

- **The bony, hollow head crests** of duckbills (hadrosaurs) may have been used for making sounds.

- **The head crests** of some hadrosaurs contained tubes called respiratory airways, which were used for breathing.

- **Air blown forcefully** through a hadrosaur's head crest passages could have made the whole crest vibrate.

- **A vibrating head crest** may have made a loud sound like a honk, roar or bellow – similar to an elephant trumpeting with its trunk.

- **Fossil skulls** of some hadrosaurs, such as *Edmontosaurus* and *Kritosaurus*, suggest that there was a loose flap of skin, like a floppy bag, between the nostrils and the eyes.

- ***Kritosaurus* may have inflated** its loose nasal flap of skin like a balloon to make a honking or bellowing sound, as some seals do today.

Tyrannosaurus

◄ *In a battle between predator and prey,* Tyrannosaurus *may have been startled or warned off by the trumpeting of Parasaurolophus.*

Parasaurolophus

Babies

- **As far as we know**, female dinosaurs laid eggs from which their babies hatched.

- **The time between** eggs being laid and babies hatching is called the incubation period.

- **Incubation periods** for dinosaur eggs probably varied by weeks or months depending on the temperature, as in today's reptiles.

▼ *Various clues from fossil evidence show that the hadrosaur* Maiasaura *may have brought food back to its newly hatched young in the nest. Whether one parent or both did this is not known.*

Hatchling

Unhatched egg

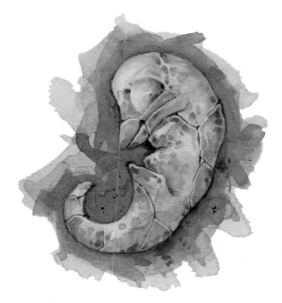

- **Many fossils** of adult *Maiasaura* have been found, together with its nests, eggs and hatchlings (newly hatched babies).

- **Fossils of *Maiasaura*** come mainly from Montana, USA.

- **The teeth of *Maiasaura*** babies found in the nest are slightly worn, suggesting that they had eaten food.

- **The leg bones and joints** of the *Maiasaura* babies were not quite fully formed, showing that they were not yet able to move about to gather their own food.

▲ *Some fossil dinosaur eggs contain preserved embryos, still in the process of development. The growing embryo would have been nourished by nutrients stored in the egg yolk inside the egg.*

- **The name** *Maiasaura* means 'good mother reptile'.

- **Evidence from *Maiasaura*** and other nesting sites shows that dinosaurs may have been caring parents, protecting and feeding their young.

Nests and eggs

🦶 **There are hundreds** of discoveries of fossil dinosaur eggs and nests, found with the parent dinosaurs.

🦶 **Eggs and nests** of the plant eater *Protoceratops*, an early kind of horned dinosaur, have been found.

🦶 **Many nests** of *Protoceratops* were found in a small area, showing that these dinosaurs bred in colonies.

🦶 **The nests were shallow**, bowl-shaped pits about one metre across, scraped in the earth.

🦶 **New nests** had been made on top of old ones, showing that the colony was used year after year.

🦶 **The eggs** were probably covered with earth and incubated by the heat of the sun.

🦶 **Some of the nests** once thought to be of *Protoceratops* are now believed to belong to *Oviraptor*.

> **DID YOU KNOW?**
> Some preserved nests of Maiasaura babies contain traces of fossil buds and leaves – perhaps food brought to them by a parent?

Nests and eggs of the plant eater *Orodromeus* have been found in Montana, USA.

In each nest, about 20 *Orodromeus* eggs were neatly arranged in a spiral, starting with one in the centre and working outwards.

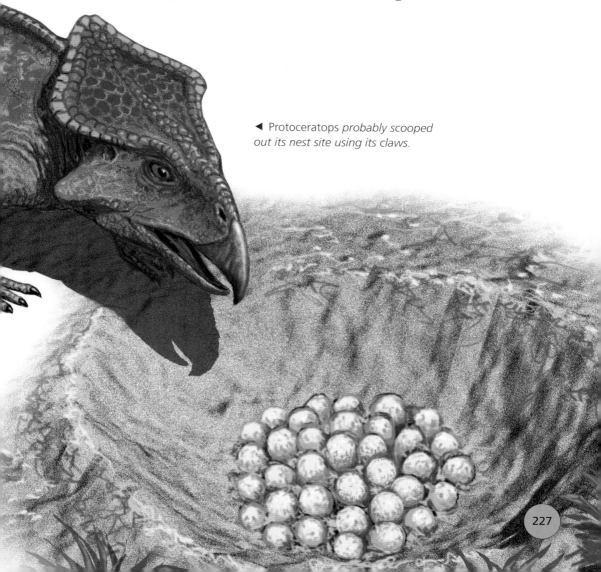

◄ Protoceratops *probably scooped out its nest site using its claws.*

227

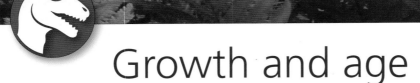

Growth and age

- **No one knows for sure** how fast dinosaurs grew, how long they took to reach adult size, or how long they lived.

- **Most estimates** of dinosaur growth rates and ages come from comparisons with today's reptiles.

- **Some reptiles today** continue to grow throughout their lives, although their growth rate slows with age.

- **Dinosaurs may have grown** fast as youngsters and slower as adults, never quite stopping until they died.

- **Estimates for the age** of an adult meat eater such as *Tyrannosaurus* range from 20 to more than 30 years.

- **Small adult meat eaters** such as *Compsognathus* may have lived to be only 3–10 years old.

- **A giant sauropod** probably lived to be 50 years old, or even more than 100 years old.

- **Like many reptiles today**, a dinosaur's growth rate probably depended largely on its food supply.

▶ Tyrannosaurus *gained 600 kg per year between the ages of 14 and 18.*

● **Dinosaurs probably ate** a lot and grew fast when food was plentiful, and slowed down when food was scarce.

● **During its lifetime**, a big sauropod such as *Brachiosaurus* would have increased its weight 2000 times (compared to 20 times in a human).

Europe

🦕 **The first dinosaur fossils** ever discovered and given official names were found in England in the 1820s.

🦕 **One of the first** almost complete dinosaur skeletons found was that of the big plant eater *Iguanodon*, in 1871, in southern England.

🦕 **Some of the most numerous** early fossils found were those of *Iguanodon*, discovered in the Belgian village of Bernissart in 1878.

🦕 **About 155–150 mya**, Solnhofen in southern Germany was a mosaic of lush islands and shallow lagoons – ideal for many kinds of life.

🦕 **At Solnhofen**, amazingly detailed fossils of tiny *Compsognathus* and the first-known bird *Archaeopteryx* have been found preserved in sandstone.

◄ *The dots indicate just a few of the dinosaur fossil sites found in Europe.*

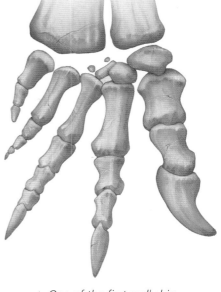

- Fossils of *Compsognathus* were also found near Nice in southern France.

- **Many fossils** of *Plateosaurus* were recovered from Trossingen, Germany, in 1911–12, 1921–23 and 1932.

- **Some of the largest fossil eggs**, measuring 30 cm long, were thought to have been laid by *Hypselosaurus* near Aix-en-Provence in southern France.

- **The Isle of Wight** off southern England has provided so many dinosaur fossils that it is sometimes known as 'Dinosaur Island'.

- Fossils of *Hypsilophodon* have been found in eastern Spain, and those of *Camptosaurus* on the coast of Portugal.

▲ One of the first really big dinosaurs was Plateosaurus, or 'flat reptile'. Its front feet could be hyper-extended. This flexibility meant that Plateosaurus *may have been able to grasp branches while feeding.*

► During the Jurassic Period, much of Europe would have looked like this. There was a much more tropical climate where ferns, ginkgoes, horsetails and cycads flourished alongside forests of conifers and tree ferns.

Africa

The first major discoveries of dinosaur fossils in Africa were made in 1907, at Tendaguru, present-day Tanzania. They included *Brachiosaurus*, *Dicraeosaurus*, and the stegosaur-like *Kentrosaurus*.

Remains of *Cetiosaurus* were found in Morocco, north Africa.

Camarasaurus, a 20-tonne plant eater, is known from fossils found in Niger, as well as from European and North American fossils.

Fossils of *Spinosaurus*, the largest meat-eating dinosaur, come from Morocco and Egypt.

The sail-backed *Ouranosaurus* is known from remains found in Niger.

▼ Jobaria *(Sahara region) and* Janenschia *(Malawi and Tanzania) are two giant sauropods recently discovered in Africa during the 1990s.*

Janenschia

Jobaria

► In Africa, as elsewhere, fossils are easier to find in places with bare, rocky soils, such as the Sahara region.

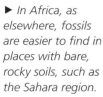

🦖 **Many sauropod fossils** were uncovered at sites in Zimbabwe, including *Barosaurus* and *Vulcanodon*.

🦖 **Remains of *Massospondylus*,** a plant-eating prosauropod, were extracted from several sites in southern Africa.

🦖 **Fossils thought to be** of *Anchisaurus* were found in southern Africa, the only site for this dinosaur outside North America.

🦖 **During the 1908–12** fossil-hunting expedition to Tendaguru, more than 250 tonnes of fossil bones and rocks from dinosaurs such as *Brachiosaurus* were carried 65 km to the nearest port, for transport to Germany.

233

Asia

🦶 **Hundreds of kinds** of dinosaurs have been discovered on the continent of Asia.

🦶 **In Asia**, most of the dinosaur fossils that have been found so far were located in the Gobi Desert in Central Asia, and in present-day China. Some were also found in present-day India.

🦶 **Remains of *Titanosaurus***, the huge plant-eating sauropod, were uncovered near Umrer, in India. It lived about 70 mya, and was similar in shape to its cousin of the same time, *Saltasaurus*, from South America.

🦶 ***Titanosaurus* was about** 12 m long and weighed 5–10 tonnes.

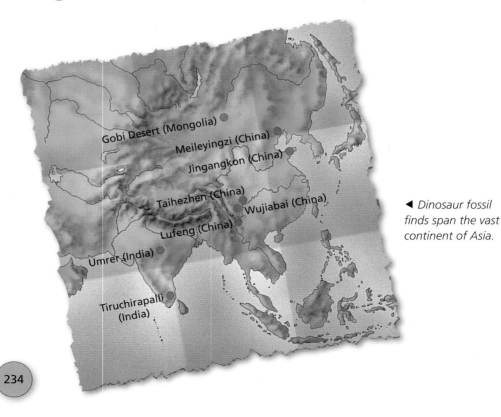

Gobi Desert (Mongolia)
Meileyingzi (China)
Jingangkon (China)
Taihezhen (China)
Wujiabai (China)
Lufeng (China)
Umrer (India)
Tiruchirapalli (India)

◀ *Dinosaur fossil finds span the vast continent of Asia.*

▲ *Fossils of* Tuojiangosaurus *come from the Sichuan area of southwest China. It was about 7 m long and is one of east Asia's best known dinosaurs.*

Fossils of the sauropod *Barapasaurus* were found in India and described and named in 1975.

Barapasaurus **was 18 m long** and probably weighed more than 20 tonnes. It is one of the first sauropods known from anywhere in the world, living around 185–175 mya.

Fossils of *Dravidosaurus*, a type of sea reptile once thought to belong to the stegosaur group, were found near Tiruchirapalli in southern India.

Gobi Desert

- **The Gobi Desert** covers much of southern Mongolia and parts of northern China.

- **The first fossil-hunting expeditions** to the Gobi Desert took place in 1922–25, and were organized by the American Museum of Natural History.

▼ Gallimimus *fossils were found in the early 1970s in the Nemegt region of the Gobi, which has yielded many exciting remains. There are parts of skeletons of many individuals, ranging from youngsters to adults.*

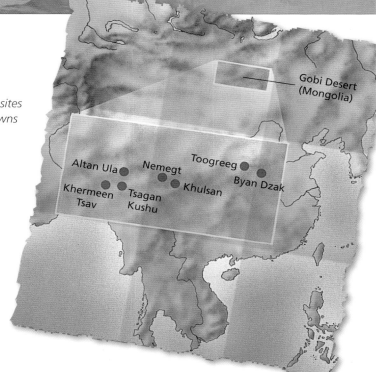

▶ The Gobi's fossil sites are far from any towns or cities.

Gobi Desert (Mongolia)

Altan Ula
Nemegt
Toogreeg
Khermeen Tsav
Tsagan Kushu
Khulsan
Byan Dzak

🐾 **The expeditions** set out to look for fossils of early humans, but instead found amazing dinosaur remains.

🐾 **The first fossil dinosaur eggs** were found by the 1922–25 expeditions.

🐾 *Velociraptor*, *Avimimus* and *Pinacosaurus* were discovered in the Gobi.

🐾 **Russian expeditions** to the Gobi Desert in 1946 and 1948–49 discovered new armoured and duckbilled dinosaurs, and the huge meat eater *Tarbosaurus*.

🐾 **More expeditions** in the 1960s–70s found the giant sauropod *Opisthocoelicaudia* and the helmet-headed *Prenocephale*.

🐾 **Other Gobi dinosaurs** include *Gallimimus* and *Oviraptor*.

237

China

- **For centuries**, dinosaur fossils in China were identified as belonging to folklore creatures such as dragons.

- **The first fossils** studied scientifically in China were uncovered in the 1930s.

- **From the 1980s**, dinosaur discoveries in almost every province of China have amazed scientists around the globe.

- **A few exciting dinosaur finds** in China have been fakes, such as part of a bird skeleton that was joined to the part-skeleton of a dinosaur along a natural-looking crack in the rock.

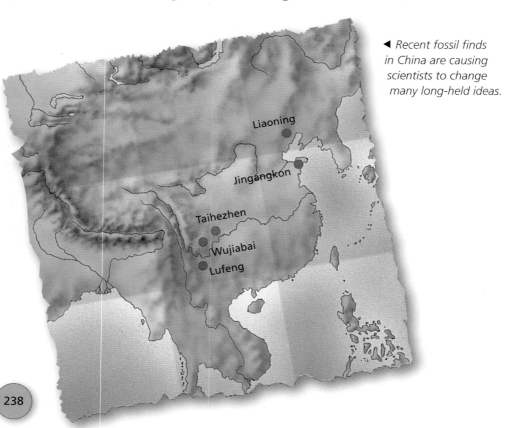

◀ Recent fossil finds in China are causing scientists to change many long-held ideas.

Liaoning

Jingangkon

Taihezhen

Wujiabai

Lufeng

◄ Microraptor gui *from the Early Cretaceous Period is the only dinosaur with feathers on its body, arms and legs. Its remains come from the Liaoning region of northeast China, which has produced some of the most amazing fossils ever discovered.*

🐾 **Some better-known Chinese finds** include *Mamenchisaurus*, *Psittacosaurus*, *Tuojiangosaurus* and *Avimimus*.

🐾 **Remains of the prosauropod** *Lufengosaurus* were uncovered in China's southern province of Yunnan, in 1941.

🐾 **China's *Lufengosaurus*** lived during the Early Jurassic Period, and measured about 6–7 m in length.

🐾 **Many recently found fossils** in China are of feathered dinosaurs such as *Caudipteryx*, *Sinosauropteryx* and *Microraptor*.

239

Australia

- **In the past 50 years**, some of the most exciting discoveries of dinosaur fossils have come from Australia.

- **Remains of the large plant eater** *Muttaburrasaurus* were found near Muttaburra, Queensland.

- **Muttaburrasaurus** was about 7 m long and similar in some ways to the well known plant eater *Iguanodon*.

- **Fossils of *Rhoetosaurus***, a giant plant eater, were found in 1924 in southern Queensland.

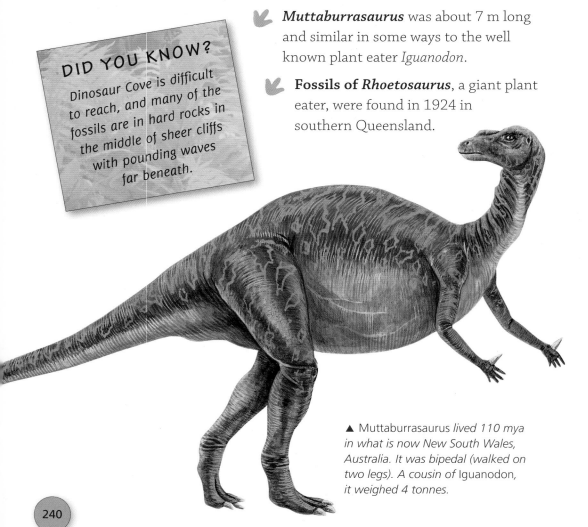

DID YOU KNOW?

Dinosaur Cove is difficult to reach, and many of the fossils are in hard rocks in the middle of sheer cliffs with pounding waves far beneath.

▲ Muttaburrasaurus *lived 110 mya in what is now New South Wales, Australia. It was bipedal (walked on two legs). A cousin of* Iguanodon, *it weighed 4 tonnes.*

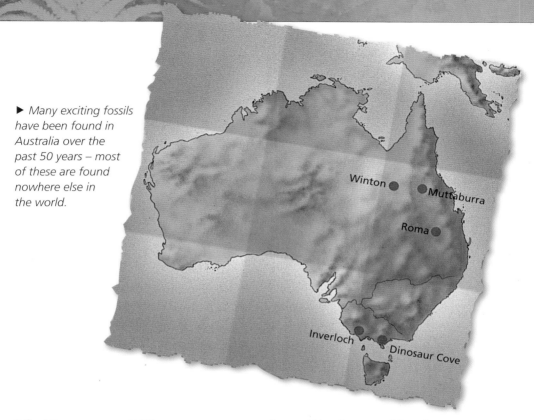

► *Many exciting fossils have been found in Australia over the past 50 years – most of these are found nowhere else in the world.*

Winton ● ● Muttaburra

Roma ●

Inverloch

Dinosaur Cove

🦶 **The sauropod Rhoetosaurus** was about 17 m long and lived 170 mya.

🦶 **Near Winton, Queensland**, more than 3300 footprints show where about 130 dinosaurs once passed by.

🦶 **One of the major fossil sites** in Australia is Dinosaur Cove, on the coast near Melbourne, Victoria.

🦶 **Fossil-rich rocks** at Dinosaur Cove are part of the Otway-Strzelecki mountain ranges, and are 120–100 million years old.

🦶 **Remains found** at Dinosaur Cove include *Leaellynasaura*, a smaller version of the huge meat eater *Allosaurus*, and the plant eater *Atlascopcosaurus*.

North America

- **North America** is the continent where most dinosaur fossils have been found.

- **Most of these fossils** come from the West region, which includes the US states of Montana, Wyoming, Utah, Colorado and Arizona and Alberta in Canada.

Colville (Alaska)

Peace River (Canada)

Bay of Fundy (Canada)

Dinosaur Provincial Park (Canada)

Mt Tom (USA)

Drumheller (Canada)

Haddonfield (USA)

Choteau (USA)

Hell Creek (USA)

Lance Creek (USA)

Billings (USA)

Como Ridge (USA)

Dinosaur Nat. Monument (USA)

Cleveland–Lloyd Dinosaur Quarry

Garden Park (USA)

San Juan River (USA)

Ghost Ranch (USA)

Paluxy River (USA)

Moreno Hills (USA)

Coahuila State (Mexico)

▲ *This map shows some of the most important fossil sites of North America. Remains of some of the most famous dinosaurs have been found at these locations, including* Allosaurus, Tyrannosaurus, Diplodocus, Triceratops *and* Stegosaurus.

▶ Coelophysis *was discovered in New Mexico, USA, in 1881. In the 1940s, another expedition found dozens of skeletons in a mass dinosaur grave.*

Several fossil-rich sites in North America are now national parks.

The US Dinosaur National Monument, on the border of Utah and Colorado, was established in 1915.

The Cleveland-Lloyd Dinosaur Quarry in Utah contains fossils of stegosaurs, ankylosaurs, sauropods and meat eaters such as *Allosaurus*.

Along the Red Deer River in Alberta, a large area with thousands of dinosaur fossils has been designated the Dinosaur Provincial Park.

Fossils found in Alberta include those of the meat eater *Albertosaurus*, armoured *Euoplocephalus* and the duckbill *Lambeosaurus*.

The Dinosaur Provincial Park in Alberta is a United Nations World Heritage Site, which means it's of outstanding natural importance.

A huge, 20-m-long plant eater was named *Alamosaurus* from the Ojo Alamo rock formations, now known as Kirtland Shales, in New Mexico, USA.

South America

- **Many of the most important** discoveries of dinosaur fossils in the last 30 years were made in South America.

- **Dinosaur fossils** have been found from the north to the south of the continent, in the countries of Brazil and Argentina.

- **Most dinosaur fossils** in South America have been found on the high grassland, scrub and semi-desert of southern Brazil and Argentina.

- **Some of the earliest known dinosaurs,** such as *Herrerasaurus* and *Eoraptor*, lived more than 225 mya in Argentina.

- **Some of the last dinosaurs**, such as the sauropods *Saltasaurus* and *Titanosaurus*, lived in Argentina.

◄ Saltasaurus *is named after the region in Argentina where its fossils were discovered, Salta Province.*

▶ Dinosaur fossils found in South America since the 1970s reveal unique kinds of meat eaters, the biggest predatory dinosaurs, some of the earliest members of the dinosaur group, and possibly the largest of all dinosaurs, Argentinosaurus.

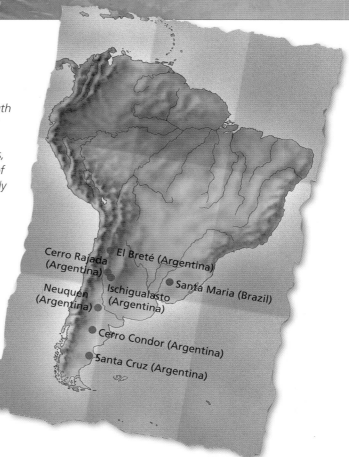

Cerro Rajada (Argentina)

El Breté (Argentina)

Neuquén (Argentina)

Ischigualasto (Argentina)

Santa Maria (Brazil)

Cerro Condor (Argentina)

Santa Cruz (Argentina)

Fossils of the meat-eating predator *Piatnitzkyosaurus* come from Cerro Condo in southern Argentina.

Piatnitzkyosaurus **was similar** to the great predator *Allosaurus* of North America, but at 4–5 m long, it was less than half its size.

Like many dinosaurs in Argentina, *Piatnitzkyosaurus* lived during the Middle Jurassic Period.

Remains of about 10 huge *Patagosaurus* sauropods were found in the fossil-rich region of Chubut, Argentina, from 1977.

245

Fossil formation

Most of the information we know, or guess, about dinosaurs comes from fossils.

Fossils are the remains of once-living things that have been preserved in rocks and turned to stone, usually over millions of years.

Many kinds of living things from prehistoric times have left fossils, including mammals, birds, lizards, fish, insects as well as plants such as ferns and trees.

The flesh, guts and other soft parts of a dead dinosaur's body were probably eaten by scavengers, or rotted away, and so they rarely formed fossils.

▼ *Fossil formation is a very long process, and extremely prone to chance and luck. Only a tiny fraction of dinosaurs that ever lived have left remains preserved by this process. Because of the way fossils are formed, dinosaurs that died in water or along banks and shores were most likely to become fossilized. It is extremely rare to find all the parts of a dinosaur arranged as they were in life.*

1 Dinosaur dies and its soft parts are scavenged or rot away

2 Sand, mud or other sediments cover the hard parts, such as the claws, teeth or bones

🐾 **Fossils usually formed** when a dinosaur's remains were quickly covered by sediments such as sand, silt or mud, especially along the banks of a river or lake, or on the seashore.

🐾 **The sand or other sediment** around a dinosaur's remains was gradually buried deeper by more sediment, squeezed under pressure, and cemented together into a solid mass of rock.

🐾 **As the sediment turned** to rock, so did the dinosaur remains encased within it.

🐾 **Information about dinosaurs** comes not only from fossils of their body parts, but also from 'trace' fossils. These were not actual parts of their bodies, but other items or signs of their presence.

🐾 **Trace fossils** include egg shells, footprints, marks made by claws and teeth, and coprolites – fossilized dinosaur droppings.

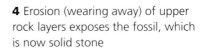

3 More layers build up as the minerals in the shell and other hard parts turn to rock

4 Erosion (wearing away) of upper rock layers exposes the fossil, which is now solid stone

Age of Dinosaurs

🦶 **The Age of Dinosaurs** corresponds to the time period that geologists call the Mesozoic Era, from about 251–65 mya.

🦶 **The Mesozoic Era** is divided into three shorter time spans – the Triassic, Jurassic and Cretaceous Periods.

🦶 **In the Triassic Period**, 251–200 mya, the dinosaurs began to evolve.

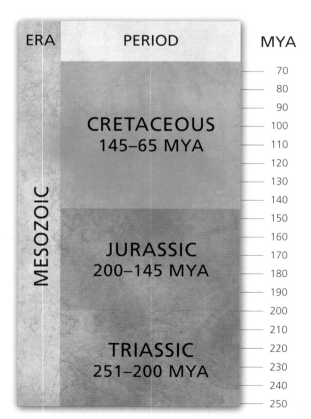

ERA	PERIOD	MYA
		— 70
		— 80
		— 90
	CRETACEOUS	— 100
	145–65 MYA	— 110
		— 120
		— 130
		— 140
M		— 150
E		— 160
S	**JURASSIC**	— 170
O	200–145 MYA	— 180
Z		— 190
O		— 200
I		— 210
C	**TRIASSIC**	— 220
	251–200 MYA	— 230
		— 240
		— 250

◄ Dinosaurs ruled the land for 185 million years – longer than any other animal group.

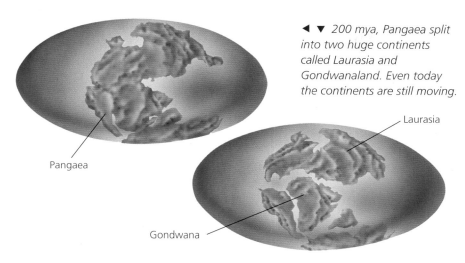

◀ ▼ 200 mya, Pangaea split into two huge continents called Laurasia and Gondwanaland. Even today the continents are still moving.

Laurasia

Pangaea

Gondwana

🐾 **During the Jurassic Period** – about 200–145 mya – the dinosaurs reached their greatest size.

🐾 **The Cretaceous Period** is when dinosaurs were at their most varied – about 145–65 mya.

🐾 **In the Triassic Period**, all the continents were joined as one supercontinent – Pangaea.

🐾 **In the Jurassic Period**, the supercontinent of Pangaea separated into two huge landmasses – Laurasia in the north and Gondwana in the south.

🐾 **In the Cretaceous Period**, Laurasia and Gondwana split, and the continents as we know them began to form.

🐾 **In the Mesozoic Era**, the major landmasses gradually moved across the globe in a process known as 'continental drift'.

🐾 **The joining and separating** of the continents affected which kinds of dinosaurs lived where.

Archosaurs

- **Archosaurs were** a large group of reptiles that included the dinosaurs as one of their subgroups.

- **Other archosaur subgroups** included thecodonts, flying reptiles called pterosaurs, and crocodiles.

- **Thecodonts included** a smaller reptile group, the ornithosuchians – possibly the dinosaurs' ancestors.

- **One of the most dinosaur-like** of the archosaurs was the thecodont *Ornithosuchus*.

- **Four-m-long** *Ornithosuchus* stood almost upright and was probably a powerful predator.

- ***Ornithosuchus* fossils** have been found in Scotland.

▶ Ornithosuchus *had a mix of features, both non-dinosaur (hips and back plates) and dinosaur (legs and skull).*

- **Features in *Ornithosuchus'*** backbone, hips and feet indicate that it was almost certainly not a dinosaur.

- ***Longisquama* was** a lizard-like archosaur only 15 cm long, with tall scales forming a V-shaped row along its back.

Inventing the dinosaur

- **When fossils of dinosaurs** were first studied by scientists in the 1820s, they were thought to be from huge lizards, rhinoceroses or even whales.

- **The first dinosaur** to be officially named in 1824 was *Megalosaurus*, by Englishman William Buckland.

- **Fossils of dinosaurs** were found and studied in 1822 by Gideon Mantell, a doctor in Sussex, southern England.

- **In 1825**, Gideon Mantell named his creature *Iguanodon*, because its teeth were very similar in shape to, but larger than, the teeth of the iguana lizard.

- **In the late 1830s**, British scientist Richard Owen realized that some fossils did not belong to lizards, but to an as yet unnamed group of reptiles.

- **In 1841–42**, Richard Owen invented a new name for the group of giant prehistoric reptiles – Dinosauria.

- **The name 'dinosaur'** means 'terrible reptile'.

- **Life-sized models** of several dinosaurs were made by British sculptor Waterhouse Hawkins in 1852–54.

- **Hawkins' models** were displayed at the Crystal Palace Exhibition in London, and caused a public sensation.

- **The three main dinosaurs** of the Dinosauria in the 1840s were *Iguanodon*, meat eater *Megalosaurus* and the nodosaur *Hylaeosaurus*.

▼ Megalosaurus *was the first dinosaur to be given an official scientific name, even though the term 'dinosaur' had not yet been invented.*

Dinosaur fossil hunters

- **Many dinosaurs** were found in the USA in the 1870s–90s by Othniel Charles Marsh and Edward Drinker Cope.

- **Marsh and Cope** were great rivals, each one trying to find bigger, better and more dinosaur fossils than the other.

- **Between 1877 and 1897**, Cope and Marsh found and described about 130 new kinds of dinosaurs.

- **Joseph Tyrrell** discovered fossils of *Albertosaurus* in 1884, in what became a very famous dinosaur region, the Red Deer River area of Alberta, Canada.

- **Lawrence Lambe** found many North American dinosaur fossils, such as *Centrosaurus* in 1904.

- **German fossil experts** Werner Janensch and Edwin Hennig led expeditions to east Africa in 1908–12, and discovered *Brachiosaurus* and *Kentrosaurus*.

- **From 1933**, Yang Zhong-jiang (also called CC Young) led many fossil hunting expeditions in China.

- **José Bonaparte** from Argentina has found many fossils in that region, including *Carnotaurus* in 1985.

DID YOU KNOW?
One of the first great fossil hunters in the USA was Joseph Leidy, who found Troodon in 1856.

◀ ▼ *Othniel Charles Marsh and Edward Drinker Cope had a rivalry between them that came to be known as the 'Bone Wars'. Allegedly, this began when Marsh pointed out a mistake that Cope had made with the reconstruction of a plesiosaur skeleton. Cope never forgave him, but the rift led to the discovery of almost 140 new dinosaur species!*

Othniel Charles Marsh
(1831–99)

Edward Drinker Cope
(1840–97)

255

Dinosaur names 1

- **Every dinosaur** has a scientific name, usually made up from Latin or Greek and written in *italics*.

- **Many dinosaur names** end in *-saurus*, which some scientists say means 'reptile' and others say means 'lizard' – but dinosaurs were not lizards.

- **Names often refer** to a unique feature a dinosaur had. *Baryonyx*, for example, means 'heavy claw', from the massive claw on its thumb.

🦶 **The meat eater** *Herrerasaurus* from Argentina was named after Victorino Herrera, the farmer who found its fossils.

🦶 **Many dinosaur names** are real tongue-twisters, such as *Opisthocoelicaudia*, pronounced 'owe-pis-thowe-see-lee-cord-ee-ah'. The name means 'posterior tail cavity', and refers to the joints between the backbones in the dinosaur's tail.

🦶 **Some dinosaurs** are named after the place where their fossils were found. Minmi was found near *Minmi* Crossing, Queensland, Australia.

🦶 **Some dinosaur groups** are named after the first discovered or major one of its kind, such as the tyrannosaurs or stegosaurs.

🦶 **The fast-running ostrich dinosaurs** are named ornithomimosaurs, which means 'bird-mimic reptiles'.

◀ *In 1988, an almost complete specimen of* Herrerasaurus *was excavated. It was named after the farmer who discovered it.*

257

Dinosaur names 2

- **More than 150 types of dinosaur** have been named after the people who first discovered their fossils, dug them up, or reconstructed the dinosaur.

- **The large duckbill (hadrosaur)** *Lambeosaurus* was named after Canadian fossil expert Lawrence Lambe.

- **Lambe worked mainly** during the early 1900s, and named one of his finds *Stephanosaurus*.

- **In the 1920s,** *Stephanosaurus* was renamed, along with *Didanodon*, as *Lambeosaurus*, in honour of Lambe's work.

- **The full name** of the 'heavy claw' meat eater *Baryonyx* is *Baryonyx walkeri*, after Bill Walker, the discoverer of its massive claw.

- **Part-time fossil hunter** Bill Walker found the claw in a clay pit quarry in Surrey, England.

▲ *The first fossil find of* Baryonyx *was its huge thumb claw.*

DID YOU KNOW?

Australian Leaellynasaura was named after Lea Ellyn, the daughter of its discoverers.

- **Some dinosaur names** are quite technical, such as *Diplodocus*, which means 'double beam'. It was named for its tail bones, which have two long projections like a pair of skis.

- **The 4-m-long plant eater** *Othnielia* was named after 19th-century fossil hunter Othniel Charles Marsh.

- ***Parksosaurus***, a 2.5-m-long plant eater, was named in honour of Canadian dinosaur expert William Parks.

▲ Alectrosaurus *means 'lonely lizard'. It lived 90–75 mya in Central Asia.*

259

Cousins: Air

- **Many flying creatures** lived during the Age of Dinosaurs, especially insects such as dragonflies, and birds.

- **The main flying creatures** were the pterosaurs, or 'winged reptiles'.

- **Hundreds of different** pterosaurs came and went through the Age of Dinosaurs, about 220–65 mya.

- **The arms of a pterosaur** resembled wings – a light, thin membrane was held out by the finger bones, especially the fourth finger.

▶ *Unlike other pterosaurs, Pteranodon had a huge head crest, which may have acted as a stabilizer during flight.*

- **Pterosaurs are sometimes** called pterodactyls, but *Pterodactylus* was just one kind of pterosaur.

- *Pterodactylus* **had** a wing span of 1–2 m. It lived 150–140 mya in southern Germany.

- **Some pterosaurs**, such as *Pteranodon*, had very short tails, or no tail at all. *Pteranodon* lived about 100 mya.

- **The pterosaur** *Rhamphorhynchus* had a long, trailing tail with a widened, paddle-shaped end.

- **Fossils suggest** that some pterosaurs, such as *Sordes*, had fur, and may have been warm-blooded, agile fliers rather than slow, clumsy gliders.

- **The biggest pterosaur**, and one of the largest flying animals ever, was *Quetzalcoatlus*. Its 'beak' was longer than an adult human, and its wings were almost 12 m across.

Cousins: Land

- **Land animals** during the Age of Dinosaurs included insects, spiders, other reptiles, birds and mammals.

- **Dinosaurs had** many fierce reptile enemies.

- **One of the biggest** non-dinosaur land reptiles was *Deinosuchus* (or *Phobosuchus*), a type of crocodile.

- ***Deinosuchus* lived** in the Late Cretaceous Period, in present-day Texas, USA.

- **The fossil skull** of *Deinosuchus* measures about 2 m long, much bigger than any crocodile of today.

▲ *Therapsids lived before the dinosaurs and also alongside the early dinosaurs.*

◀ Erythrosuchus *was a crocodile that lived 240 mya. It was 4.4 m long and lived in swamps.*

- *Protosuchus*, an early type of crocodile, moved nimbly on its upright legs, and its mouth had wide, powerful jaws.

- **The first mammals** appeared about the same time as the early dinosaurs.

- **Mammals lived** throughout the Age of Dinosaurs, but none grew larger than a badger, at about one metre long.

- **One of the first mammals** was *Megazostrodon*, which resembled a shrew of today. Its fossils, from 220–210 mya, come from southern Africa.

DID YOU KNOW?

Thecodonts were slim, long-legged reptiles that lived just before the dinosaurs. They probably caught bugs and lizards to eat.

263

Cousins: Sea

Placodonts were marine reptiles that lived mainly during the Triassic Period. They were shaped like large salamanders or turtles, and probably ate shellfish.

Placodus **was** a 2-m-long placodont that looked like a large, scaly newt.

▼ The nostrils and eyes of Mastodonsaurus *were on top of its head so that it could breathe and look around whilst hiding underwater.*

- *Nothosaurs* **were fish-eating reptiles** of the Triassic Period. They had small heads, long necks and tails, and four flipper-shaped limbs.

- **Fossils of *Nothosaurus*,** a 3-m-long nothosaur, have been found across Europe, Asia and Africa.

- **The dolphin-like ichthyosaurs** had back fins, two-lobed tails and flipper-shaped limbs.

- **Many kinds of ichthyosaurs** thrived in the seas during the Triassic and Jurassic Periods, although they had faded away by the middle of the Cretaceous Period.

- **One of the biggest** ichthyosaurs was *Shonisaurus*, which measured up to 15 m long.

- **The plesiosaurs** were fish-eating reptiles of the Mesozoic Era. They had small heads, tubby bodies, four flipper-shaped limbs and short, tapering tails.

- **Mosasaurs were a group** of large, fierce sea reptiles that appeared between 160–120 mya.

DID YOU KNOW?

One of the biggest meat eaters ever was the plesiosaur Liopleurodon. It was possibly 20 m long and weighed a staggering 50 tonnes.

Extinction

All dinosaurs on Earth had died out, or become extinct, by 65 mya.

Many other reptiles, such as mosasaurs and plesiosaurs, along with pterosaurs and other animals and plants, disappeared with the dinosaurs in a mass extinction.

A possible cause of this extinction was a new kind of disease that swept across the land and seas.

One theory is that a series of huge volcanic eruptions filled the air with poisonous fumes.

Climate change is another possible cause of mass extinction – perhaps a period of global warming that lasted for a few hundred years, or even longer.

▼ *The last dinosaurs, such as* Triceratops *and* Tyrannosaurus *may have been engulfed by a massive meteorite impact that set off wildfires, volcanoes and tsunamis (tidal waves) – and ultimately blocked out the Sun.*

DID YOU KNOW?

Scientists have found a huge crater – the Chixulub Crater – under seabed mud off the coast of Yucatan, Mexico. This could be where a giant meteorite hit the Earth 65 mya.

- **Another theory** is that a giant lump of rock from space – a meteorite – collided with the Earth.

- **A giant meteorite** 10 km across would have set off earthquakes and volcanoes across the Earth, and thrown up vast amounts of dust to darken the skies and block out the Sun.

- **Lack of sunlight** for one year or more would mean that many plants died, which in turn would cause the death of plant-eating animals, and consequently the meat eaters.

- **One great puzzle** about the disappearance of the dinosaurs is why similar reptiles, such as crocodiles, lizards and turtles, survived.

After the dinosaurs

- **The Age of Dinosaurs** came to a fairly sudden end 65 mya. We know this from rocks and fossils, which changed dramatically at that time.

- **The Cretaceous Period** ended 65 mya, and there are no dinosaur fossils since this time.

- **Many animal groups**, including fish, crocodiles, turtles, lizards, birds and mammals, survived the extinction that took place 65 mya.

- **Birds and mammals** in particular underwent rapid changes after the dinosaurs disappeared.

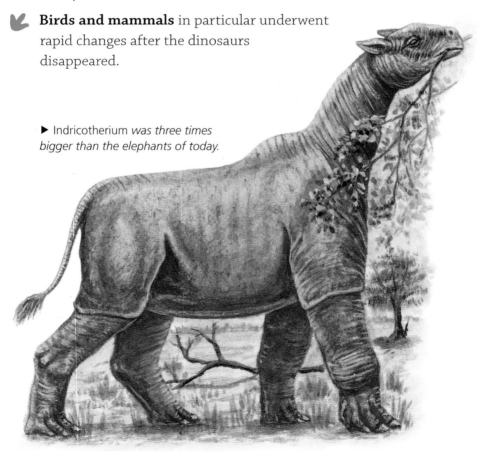

▶ Indricotherium *was three times bigger than the elephants of today.*

▶ *Fossils of the first bird were mistaken for a dinosaur.* Archaeopteryx *lived in Europe about 155 mya. Some of its fossils look very similar to the fossils of small dinosaurs. So* Archaeopteryx *was thought to be a dinosaur, until scientists saw the faint shape of its feathers and realized it was a bird.*

The land mammal that came closest to rivalling the great size of the dinosaurs was *Indricotherium*, also known as *Baluchitherium*.

***Indricotherium* was 8 m long,** 5 m tall and weighed perhaps 20 tonnes. Despite this, it was still less than one-third of the size of the biggest dinosaurs.

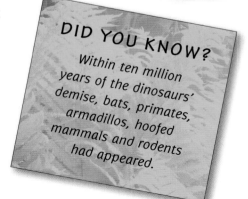

DID YOU KNOW?
Within ten million years of the dinosaurs' demise, bats, primates, armadillos, hoofed mammals and rodents had appeared.

Mysteries

🐾 **Some dinosaurs have been named** on very scant evidence, such as a single bit of fossil bone, or just one tooth or claw.

🐾 **The first tooth** of meat-eating *Troodon* was found in the Judith River region of Montana, USA.

🐾 **At first**, the *Troodon* tooth was thought to have come from a lizard.

🐾 **In the early 1900s**, more *Troodon*-like teeth were found in Alberta, Canada and Wyoming, USA. They were believed to have come from a pachycephalosaur or 'bone-head' dinosaur.

🐾 **In the 1980s**, a fuller picture of *Troodon* was built up by putting its teeth together with other fossils.

🐾 *Therizinosaurus*, or 'scythe reptile', was a huge dinosaur known only from a few parts of its limbs. It lived in the Late Cretaceous Period in Mongolia, Central Asia.

🐾 **A mysterious fossil claw** thought possibly to belong to *Therizinosaurus* has been found. It measures about 90 cm around its outer curve.

🐾 **In recent years**, fossils of several types of therizinosaurs have been found in Asia, especially in China.

🐾 **Some of these strange** dinosaurs were as tall as a giraffe, weighed more than an elephant and were probably plant eaters. They had feathery coverings over parts of their bodies.

▼ *The small meat eater* Troodon *was named in 1856 on the evidence of a single tooth.*

Reconstructions

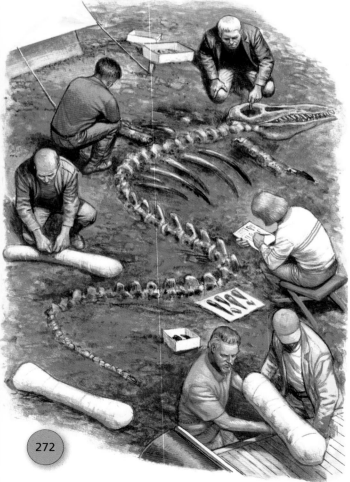

No complete fossilized dinosaur, with its skin, muscles, guts and other soft body parts, has ever been found.

Most dinosaurs are reconstructed from the fossils of their teeth, bones, horns and claws.

The vast majority are known from only a few fossil parts, such as several fragments of bones.

Fossil parts of other, similar dinosaurs are often used in reconstructions to 'fill in' missing bones, teeth, and even missing heads, limbs or tails.

Soft body parts from modern reptiles, such as lizards, are used as a guide for the reconstruction of a dinosaur's muscles and guts.

◄ These are palaeontologists, scientists that look for and study dinosaur bones, uncovering a new skeleton.

▼ At a fossil site or 'dig', scientists record every stage of excavation with measurements, maps, photographs and sketches.

▼ Some fragile fossils are wrapped in plaster bandages. These harden to support and protect the remains so that they can be moved.

On rare occasions, remains are found of a dinosaur body that dried out rapidly so that quite a few parts were preserved as mummified fossils.

One of the best known part-mummified dinosaur fossils is 'Sue', a specimen of *Tyrannosaurus* found in 1990 in South Dakota, USA. Sue is the biggest and one of the most complete preserved *Tyrannosaurus* ever found.

Probably female, Sue was named after her discoverer, fossil hunter Susan Hendrickson of the Black Hills Institute of Geological Research.

DID YOU KNOW?
'Sue', the part-mummified Tyrannosaurus, was sold in 1997 for more than $8.3 million to the Field Museum, Chicago, USA.

273

Age of mammals

Bird fossils

- **There are far fewer** fossils of birds than other animals because birds have very delicate skeletons.

- **Some species** of prehistoric birds are only revealed by the fossil impression of a feather or a fossilized footprint.

- **One of** the most famous bird fossils is that of *Archaeopteryx*, which was discovered in Solnhofen, Germany, in 1861.

- **Lime-rich muds** slowly formed the limestone rock of Solnhofen. This process ensured *Archaeopteryx* was preserved in amazing detail, right down to the clear outline of its feathers.

- **Other famous** bird fossil sites have included the Niobrara Chalk of Kansas, and mudstone rocks of Utah and Wyoming.

- **The fossil site** at Messel in Germany also contains the skeletons of long-extinct birds as well as ones resembling flamingos, swifts, owls and nightjars.

- **The Messel bird fossils** are around 50 million years old and date from the Early Tertiary Period.

- **Flamingo fossils** at Messel proved that the modern flamingo is related to wading birds called avocets rather than ducks and storks, since they share a similar skeleton.

- **One quick way** fossil hunters can identify bird bones is because they are hollow – unlike the bones of many prehistoric reptiles.

DID YOU KNOW?
An example of a fossilized egg is one belonging to the giant extinct ostrich, Aepyornis. The egg was also huge – it could hold 8.5 litres of liquid!

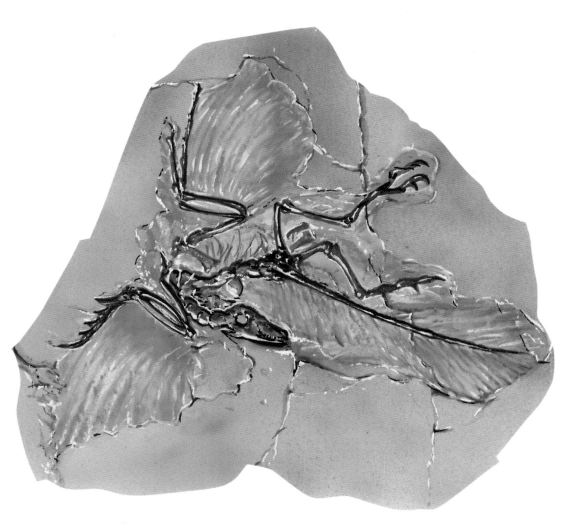

▲ *Fossils of Archaeopteryx are some of the most famous fossils of all. They show the bird's feathers, clawed fingers, teeth-filled beak and long tail.*

Terror birds

🐾 **After the dinosaurs** became extinct (about 65 mya), huge flightless birds – known as terror birds – seized the opportunity to become the dominant predators of their day.

🐾 *Gastornis* was one such terror bird. It had an enormous head and powerful legs, like those of its dinosaur ancestors, so it could outrun its prey.

🐾 **Some experts** believe that *Gastornis* is the ancestor of ducks, geese and other related birds.

🐾 **Even though these birds** could be huge, they were also light-footed, quick runners. This is because, like all birds, they had hollow bones.

🐾 **The diets** of terror birds included small and medium-sized mammals, such as prehistoric rodents and horses.

◄ Gastornis *was about 2 m tall, with a head the size of a horse's. Around 50 mya it was one of the top hunters in Europe and North America.*

▶ *The terror bird* Titanis *roamed the plains of what is now Texas and Florida about 2 mya. There is some evidence that these great birds may have survived in small numbers until humans arrived in the Americas some 30,000 years ago.*

During the Late Eocene and Oligocene Epochs (40–24 mya), the big carnivorous mammals became more powerful and better hunters and so more dominant, taking over.

However, in South America, which was cut off from North America and the rest of the world for much of the Tertiary Period (65–1.6 mya), terror birds managed to stay dominant for a longer period of time.

One South American terror bird was *Phorusrhacus*, which grew up to 1.5 m tall.

Titanis was another South American terror bird, and the biggest of all – it was 2.5 m tall and weighed 150 kg.

DID YOU KNOW?

Unlike other flightless birds, Titanis had clawed fingers at the end of its fore-limbs. It probably used these fingers for seizing its prey.

279

Other flightless birds

- **Most prehistoric** flightless birds were giants, but not all of them were terror birds.

- *Shuvuuia*, which lived about 80 mya, was an early, flightless bird. Like the terror birds, it was very large.

- *Shuvuuia* was about one metre high. It probably fed on insects and small reptiles.

- **The name** *Shuvuuia* comes from the Mongolian word for 'bird'. It lived on the plains of Central Asia and had the long, thin legs of a fast runner.

- **For a long time**, palaeontologists thought that *Shuvuuia* was a reptile, but in fact its skull is much more similar to a modern bird's than a reptile's.

- **Much later giant** birds grew to incredible sizes. *Dinornis*, for instance, was the tallest flightless bird ever at 3.5 m tall.

- *Dinornis* lived in New Zealand. It first appeared about 2 mya and survived until 300 years ago!

- **At 450 kg**, *Aepyornis* was the heaviest bird ever to have lived. It lived on the island of Madagascar between 2 million and 500 years ago.

- **Both *Dinornis* and *Aepyornis*** were herbivores. Their diet consisted of seeds and fruit.

DID YOU KNOW?

Dinornis was a type of moa bird. The only survivor of this group is the kiwi.

Emu

Ostrich

Rhea

Bennet's cassowary   Kiwi   Cassowary

▲ *These modern flightless birds are descendants of prehistoric flightless birds. The collective name for flightless birds is ratites, from the Latin* ratis *meaning 'raft'. Unlike flying birds, ratites have flat, raftlike breastbones that cannot support the muscles needed for flight.*

Water birds

- *Ichthyornis* was a prehistoric seagull, which first appeared in the Late Cretaceous Period (100–65 mya).

- **It was similar in size** to a modern seagull, but had a much larger head and a beak full of very sharp teeth.

- *Presbyornis* was a prehistoric duck. Like *Ichthyornis*, it evolved in the Late Cretaceous Period and was abundant in the Early Tertiary Period (65–40 mya).

- *Presbyornis* was much bigger than a modern duck – it stood between 0.5 m and 1.5 m tall.

- **It had much longer legs** than its modern relative and so may have been a wading bird rather than a diving bird.

- *Presbyornis* lived in large flocks on lake shores, like modern flamingos.

- *Osteodontornis* was a huge flying bird, with a wingspan up to 5.2 m across.

- **It lived in the Miocene Epoch** (23–5 mya) and would have flown over the North Pacific Ocean.

- *Osteodontornis* had a long bill, lined with toothlike bony spikes. Its diet probably included squid, seized from the surface of the sea.

▲ *Some experts believe that Palaelodus was a prehistoric flamingo that lived in France about 26 mya.*

Land birds

- **Land birds** are flying birds that fly in the skies over land and hunt or feed on the ground, unlike water birds.

- **Fossils** of prehistoric land birds are rare because their bones were light and would not have fossilized well.

- **As a result**, there are big gaps in palaeontologists' knowledge of the evolution of many species of birds. However, there are some early land birds they do know about.

- *Archaeopsittacus* was an early parrot of the Late Oligocene Epoch (28–24 mya).

- *Ogygoptynx* was the first known owl. It lived in the Palaeocene Epoch (65–58 mya).

- *Aegialornis* was an early swiftlike bird, which lived in the Eocene and Oligocene Epochs (58–24 mya). It may be the ancestor of swifts and hummingbirds.

◄ *No one knows for certain when parrots first evolved, but fossils date back to at least 20 mya. Some bird experts think that parrots were once much more plentiful than they are today.*

284

▶ This vulture's earliest ancestors were the very first birds of prey. Scientists think that Lithornis, a bird of prey that lived around 65 mya, was a type of vulture.

Gallinuloides was an early member of the chicken family. *Gallinuloides* fossils have been found in Wyoming, USA, in rock strata of the Eocene Epoch (58–37 mya).

The earliest known vultures lived in the Palaeocene Epoch (65–58 mya).

The earliest known hawks, cranes, bustards, cuckoos and songbirds lived in the Eocene Epoch.

DID YOU KNOW?
Neocathartes was an early vulture-like bird. There are similarities between its skeleton and that of storks, which suggests vultures and storks are closely related.

Mammal fossils

◀ *Fur is still visible around the feet of Dima, the baby mammoth.*

🐾 **There are few fossil** remains of the earliest mammals because scavengers would usually have eaten their bodies.

🐾 **However, coprolites** (fossilized dung) of predators and scavengers sometimes contain undigested parts of the early mammals themselves, such as their teeth.

🐾 **Palaeontologists** can tell a lot from a mammal's molar (cheek tooth). They can work out its species and the period it lived in from the pattern of ridges and furrows on its surface.

🐾 **Palaeontologists** can also estimate the age of a mammal when it died by looking at the wear and tear on its teeth.

🐾 **Some mammals** are preserved in tar pits – prehistoric pools that were full of a mixture of hydrocarbons that formed sticky tar, which preserved fossils.

🐾 **Tar pits** at Rancho La Brea, near present-day downtown Los Angeles, USA, contained a perfectly preserved skeleton of the sabre-tooth carnivore *Smilodon*.

🐾 **Freezing** is another very effective way of preserving animals. Remains of frozen mammoths have been discovered in near-perfect conditions in Siberia.

● **Explorers** using dog sledges discovered some of the first frozen mammoths. Their remains were so well preserved that the dogs were able to eat the meat on their bones.

● **The most complete** frozen mammoth find occurred in 1977, with the discovery of the 40,000-year-old baby male mammoth, which people named Dima.

● **Fossil finds** of prehistoric mammals include skulls, teeth, jawbones, ear bones, horns, tusks and antlers.

▼ *The remains of a woolly mammoth, preserved in frozen soil. Besides bones, palaeontologists have discovered skin, hair and other body parts of mammoths in Siberia.*

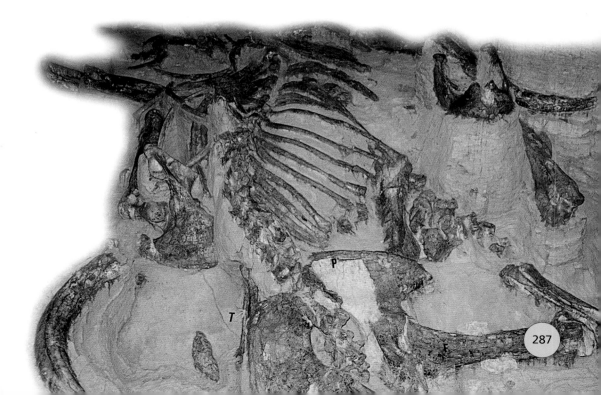

Mammal offspring

Mammals developed a very different way of producing young, compared to reptiles and birds, which both lay eggs.

Instead, most mammals are viviparous, which means they give birth to live young.

◀ *All mammal offspring, such as this lamb, feed on their mother's milk, which contains a rich source of nutrients to help them to grow quickly.*

One unusual group of mammals, the monotremes, defy this rule by laying eggs. There are five surviving monotremes – the duck-billed platypus and four species of echidna.

After the young of mammals are born, their mothers feed them milk that is produced in their mammary glands.

The word 'mammal' comes from the mammary glands – the part of female mammals' bodies that secretes milk.

- **The first mammals,** such as *Megazostrodon*, *Eozostrodon* and *Morganucodon*, grew one set of milk teeth, which suggests that the young fed on breast milk.

- **Milk teeth** are temporary teeth that grow with the nutrients provided by milk, and prepare the jaw for later teeth.

- **Mammals** can be divided into three groups depending on how they rear their young – placentals, marsupials and monotremes.

- **In placental mammals,** the offspring stays inside its mother's body, in the womb, until it is a fully developed baby – at which point it is born.

- **Marsupial mammals** give birth to their offspring at a much earlier stage. The tiny infants then develop fully in their mothers' pouch, called a marsupium.

▶ *Marsupial mammals, such as this kangaroo and its joey (infant), give birth at an earlier stage than other mammals.*

289

Early mammals

- *Megazostrodon* was one of the first true mammals. It appeared at the start of the Early Jurassic Period (about 200 mya).

- **It was a shrewlike insectivore** (insect eater) and about 12 cm long. It had a long body that was low to the ground and long limbs that it held out to the side in a squatting position.

- *Eozostrodon* was another very early mammal, which emerged about the same time as *Megazostrodon*.

- **It had true mammalian teeth**, including two different sorts of cheek teeth – premolars and molars – which were replaced only once during its lifetime.

- **Its sharp teeth** suggest it was a meat eater, and its large eyes suggest that it hunted at night.

- **A further early mammal** was *Morganucodon*. It too had premolars and molars and chewed its food in a roundabout motion, rather than the up-down motion of reptiles.

- *Sinoconodon* was yet another early mammal that lived in the Early Jurassic Period (about 200 mya). It was probably covered in fur.

- **These early mammals** had three middle ear bones, which made their hearing more sensitive than reptiles.

- **They also had whiskers**, which suggests they had fur and in turn suggests they were warm-blooded.

- **All true mammals** are warm-blooded, which means they maintain a constant body temperature. Fur helps mammals keep warm when it is cold – at night, for instance.

▲ *Like other small, early mammals,* Megazostrodon *was probably a nocturnal animal, coming out to hunt at night.*

Marsupials

Marsupials are mammals that give birth to their offspring at a very early stage in their development – when they are still tiny.

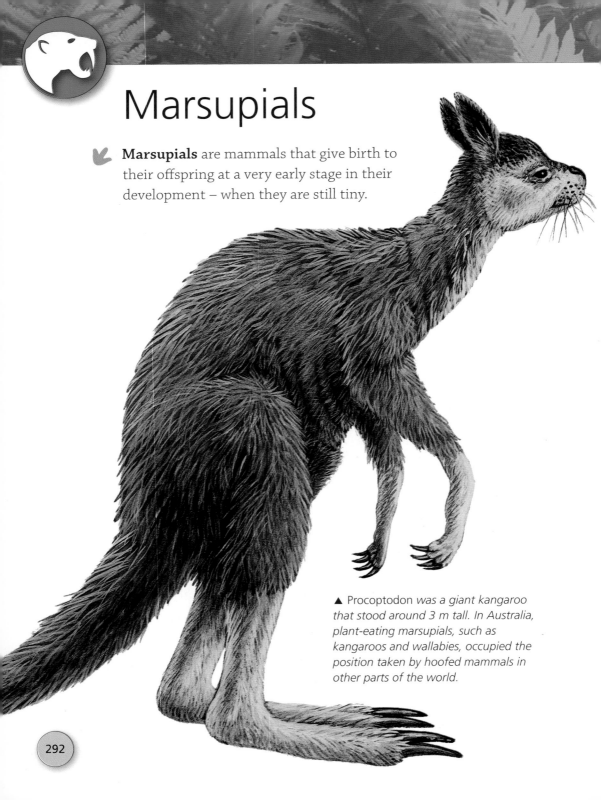

▲ Procoptodon *was a giant kangaroo that stood around 3 m tall. In Australia, plant-eating marsupials, such as kangaroos and wallabies, occupied the position taken by hoofed mammals in other parts of the world.*

- **After being born**, the infant crawls through its mother's fur to a pouch called the marsupium, where it stays, feeding on milk, until it is big enough to leave.

- **Palaeontologists** think that the first marsupials evolved in North America and then spread to South America and Australia.

- **An early marsupial** called *Alphadon,* meaning 'first tooth', emerged around 70 mya. It lived in North and South America.

- *Alphadon* **was 30 cm long** and weighed 300 g. It would have lived in trees, using its feet to climb, and fed on insects, fruit and small vertebrates.

- **When Australia** became isolated from the rest of the world about 40 mya, its marsupials continued to evolve – unlike the rest of the world, where they fell into decline.

- **Marsupials** continued to exist in South America, which was also isolated from the rest of the world, during much of the Tertiary Period (65–1.6 mya).

- **When South America** became reconnected with North America, about 3 mya, the arrival of placental mammals from the north led many marsupials to become extinct.

- **Today**, there are only two surviving groups of marsupials in the Americas: the opossums found throughout America and the rat opossums found in South America.

- **Australia** has many living marsupials, from kangaroos to koalas. However it had a much greater marsupial population in the Tertiary Period – we know this from fossil sites such as Riversleigh in northwest Queensland.

Australian mammals

- **Australia** has a unique natural history because it became isolated from the rest of the world around 40 mya.

- **Australia's native mammals**, living and extinct, are mostly marsupials – mammals that give birth to tiny young, which then develop in their mother's outside pouch.

- **The earliest Australian marsupials** date from the Oligocene Epoch (37–24 mya). Most fossils come from the Miocene Epoch (23–5 mya) or later.

- **These fossils** show that there were giant kangaroos, called *Procoptodon*, as well as giant wombats, called *Diprotodon*.

- **Two marsupial carnivores** preyed on these giant herbivores. One was the lionlike *Thylacoleo*, the other was the smaller, wolflike *Thylacinus*.

- **Palaeontologists** are very interested in *Thylacoleo* and *Thylacinus* because they both demonstrate how different species can come to look very similar – the process known as evolutionary convergence.

- **Although they had different** ancestors and lived on different continents, *Thylacoleo* came to look like a placental lion, while *Thylacinus* came to look like a placental wolf.

- **The Miocene fossil site** in Riversleigh, northern Queensland, has revealed the extent and variety of prehistoric marsupials in Australia.

● **Among the fossils** are many long-extinct marsupials. One of these was so unusual that at first palaeontologists called it a 'thingodont', although now it is known as *Yolkaparidon*.

● *Thylacinus* continued to exist in Australia into the 20th century, but the last one died in a zoo in Tasmania in 1936.

▼ *At 3.4 m long, the giant wombat* Diprotodon *was the largest marsupial ever to have lived. It had tusks for its front teeth, but its cheek teeth were like a kangaroo's.*

South American mammals

🐾 **South America** was separated from the rest of the world for much of the Tertiary Period (65–1.6 mya).

🐾 **Like Australia**, South America's isolation meant that certain mammals evolved there and nowhere else.

🐾 **The main difference** between them was that South America had placental mammals as well as marsupials.

🐾 **Placental mammals** included the giant ground sloths, such as *Megatherium*, and huge rodents the size of bears.

🐾 **Marsupial mammals** included the marsupial carnivores, such as *Thylacosmilus*.

🐾 **Evolutionary convergence**, whereby different species can come to look very similar, happened in South America just as in Australia. One example was *Thoatherium*, which looked very much like the small horses that were evolving in other parts of the world.

🐾 **The formation** of the Panama isthmus (a strip of land) reconnected South America to North America about 3 mya.

DID YOU KNOW?

An example of evolutionary convergence was the Pyrotherium, which had the trunk, cheek teeth and tusks of an early elephant – except that it wasn't one!

Many South American mammals journeyed north. Some, such as armadillos, porcupines and guinea pigs, were very successful in their new homes.

Others, like the glyptodonts, eventually died out. This might be because of climate change – or because humans hunted them to extinction.

▼ The South American hoofed mammal Macrauchenia was able to eat grass or to browse on the leaves of trees and bushes, using its trunk to gather food. It lived about 300,000 years ago.

Credonts

- **Creodonts** were the first flesh-eating mammals. They lived in the Eocene Period (58–37 mya).

- **These mammals came in many different shapes** and sizes. Some were as small as weasels, others were bigger than bears.

- **Many creodonts** were flat-footed and walked on short, heavy limbs tipped with claws.

- **They caught early herbivores** that, like these early carnivores, had not yet evolved into quick runners.

- **Creodonts had smaller**, more primitive brains than later carnivores – these were cleverer, faster hunters than the creodonts, and forced them into decline.

- **Another way** in which creodonts were less successful than later carnivores was with their teeth, which were less effective at stabbing or slicing.

- **Creodonts were**, however, the top predators of their day. The wolf-sized *Hyaenodon* was particularly successful.

DID YOU KNOW?
Hyaenodon species ranged in size from 30 cm high at the shoulders to 1.2 m high – the size of a small rhinoceros.

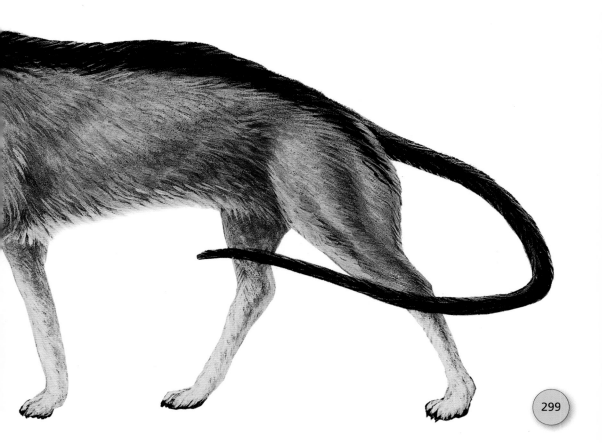

🐾 **Fossils of *Hyaenodon* skulls** show that they had a very highly developed sense of smell, as well as powerful, bone-crushing jaws.

🐾 **Fossils of male *Hyaenodon*** teeth reveal grinding marks, which palaeontologists think means they ground their teeth to ward off rivals, like some modern animals.

▼ Sinopa *was a creodont – an early carnivore. It would have been a little bigger than a domestic cat.*

Carnivores

- **The first carnivorous mammals** were the creodonts, which ranged in size from the catlike *Oxyaena* to the wolflike *Mesonyx*.

- **In the Late Eocene Epoch** (around 40 mya) large hoofed carnivores began to appear, such as *Andrewsarchus*.

- **Modern carnivores** are descended from a seperate group called miacids.

- **Modern carnivores** belong to the order Carnivora. This order had two subgroups – the fissipeds, which include the cat and dog families and the pinnipeds (seals, sea lions and walruses). Now many classification schemes put pinnipeds in their own mammal group, seperate from the fissiped carnivores.

- **In the Oligocene Epoch** (37–24 mya), fissipeds began to replace creodonts as the dominant carnivores.

- **Fissipeds** were smarter, faster, and deadlier than creodonts, and were the only predators that could catch the new fast-running herbivores.

- **Faster mammals** evolved in the Oligocene Epoch as thick forests changed into open woodlands, with more space to run after, and run from, other creatures.

- **As carnivores evolved**, so they developed bigger brains, more alert senses, sharper claws and teeth, and stronger jaws and limbs.

- **The pinnipeds** are carnivorous mammals that, like whales and dolphins (and reptiles before them), reinvaded the seas.

DID YOU KNOW?
Allodesmus was a prehistoric seal. It had flippers, large eyes and spiky teeth, which it used to impale slippery fish.

▼ Dinictis *was a fissiped carnivore and member of the cat family, which lived in North America about 30 mya. Fissipeds were superbly adapted for hunting fast-running mammals.*

Cats

- **The most highly developed** carnivores are cats. They are the fastest and most intelligent land hunters, with the sharpest claws and teeth.

- **Cats evolved** along two lines. One group was the sabre-tooths, which included *Smilodon*. This group is extinct today.

- **Sabre-tooths** specialized in killing large, heavily-built animals with thick hides, which explains their long canine teeth.

- **The other group** of cats is the felines, which are the ancestors of all modern cats, from lions and cheetahs to pet cats.

- **The felines** were faster and more agile than the sabre-tooths, who became extinct because their prey became faster and able to outrun them. The felines, however, continued to be successful hunters.

- **One prehistoric feline** was *Dinictis*, a puma-sized cat that lived in the Oligocene Epoch (37–24 mya).

- **A later feline** was *Dinofelis*, which lived between 5 and 1.4 mya.

- **The name *Dinofelis*** means 'terrible cat'. It looked like a modern jaguar, but had stronger front legs that it used to press down on its victims before stabbing them with its teeth.

- ***Dinofelis*' diet** included baboons, antelope and australopithecines – our human ancestors.

▼ The cave lion was a predator of the ice ages, attacking deer, young mammoths and rhinoceroses. It was closely related to the modern lion, but was considerably larger, standing about 1.8 m tall. It is thought to have survived in southern Europe until about 4000 years ago.

DID YOU KNOW?

Prehistoric cats' ability to unsheathe and retract their claws provided them with one of their deadliest weapons – and one that cats still have.

Dogs

- **Early dogs** hunted in a similar way to modern wild dogs – in packs.

- **Dogs developed** long snouts, which gave them a keen sense of smell, and forward-pointing eyes, which gave them good vision.

- **Dogs** also developed a mixture of teeth – sharp canines for stabbing, narrow cheek teeth for slicing and farther along the jaw, flatter teeth for crushing.

- **These different teeth** meant that dogs could eat a variety of different foods, including plants, which they might have had to eat if meat was in short supply.

- **One of the ancestors** of dogs, as well as bears, was the bear-dog *Amphicyon*. Its name means 'in-between dog'.

- *Amphicyon* lived between 40 and 9 mya.

- **Trace fossils** of *Amphicyon's* footprints show that it walked like a bear with its feet flat on the ground.

- *Hesperocyon* was one of the earliest dogs, living between 37 and 29 mya.

- *Hesperocyon* was the size of a small fox. It had long legs and jaws, forward-pointing eyes and a supple, slender body.

DID YOU KNOW?

Hunting in packs allowed Hesperocyon to catch large animals that it would not have been able to kill on its own.

▲ *Part of a pack of* Hesperocyon *dogs, tracking the scent of their prey. Organized hunting in packs is an example of dogs' intelligence.*

Herbivores

- **The first specialist herbivores** (plant eaters) appeared in the Late Palaeocene Epoch (around 60 mya).

- **They ranged in size** from the equivalent of modern badgers to pigs.

- **These early herbivores** were rooters or browsers – they foraged for food on the floors of their forest homes.

- **It was not until** the very end of the Palaeocene Epoch (58 mya) that the first large herbivores evolved.

- **Large herbivores** emerged before large carnivores. They must have had a peaceful life – for a while!

- *Uintatherium* was one of the large early herbivores. It was the size of a large rhinoceros, with thick limbs to support its heavy body.

- *Uintatherium* had three pairs of bony knobs protruding from its head. Males had very long, strong canine teeth, which they would have used if attacked by creodont carnivores.

- **The growth of grasslands** and the decline of forests in the Miocene Epoch (23–5 mya) speeded up changes to herbivores' bodies.

- **Herbivores developed** faster legs to outrun carnivores in open spaces. They also developed better digestive systems to cope with the new, tough grasses.

- **The most important** requirements for a herbivore are complex teeth and digestive systems to break down plant food and release its energy.

◀ Uintatherium *was one of a group of similar animals, all of which had a massive body, pillar-like legs and long skulls adorned with bony knobs. The entire Uintatheriidae family died out about 35 mya, perhaps because of competition from more advanced browsing mammals.*

307

Rodents

🐾 **In terms of their numbers**, variety and distribution, rodents are the most successful mammals that have ever lived.

🐾 **Squirrels**, rats, guinea pigs, beavers, porcupines, voles, gophers and mice are all types of rodent.

▲ Platypittamys *was a prehistoric, ratlike rodent. Rodents became plentiful during the Oligocene Epoch (37–24 mya).*

- **Rodents** have been – and still are – so successful because they are small, fast-breeding and able to digest all kinds of foods, including substances as hard as wood.

- **The first known rodent** was *Paramys*, which appeared about 60 mya.

- *Paramys* was a squirrel-like rodent that could climb trees. It was 60 cm long, and had a long, slightly bushy tail.

- **Modern squirrels** evolved from *Paramys* around 38 mya. These mammals have one of the longest ancestries that we know of.

- **Another early rodent** was *Epigaulus*, which was a gopher with two horns.

- *Epigaulus* was 26 cm long and lived in North America in the Miocene Epoch (23–5 mya). It probably used its horns for defence or digging up roots.

- **Prehistoric rodents** could be massive. *Castoroides* was an early beaver that was over 2 m long – almost the size of a black bear.

DID YOU KNOW?
Rabbits and hares are descended from rodents. Modern hares first appeared around 5 mya.

Ruminants

- **Ruminants** are a very successful group of plant-eating mammals that first appeared about 40 mya.

- **Modern ruminants** include cattle, sheep, deer, giraffes, antelopes and camels.

- **All these animals** can eat quickly, store plant material in the stomach, and then bring it back to their mouths again to chew it and break it down. This process is called 'chewing the cud'.

- *Archaeomeryx* was an early, rabbit-sized ruminant, which lived in Asia. It is the ancestor of the chevrotain – a small, hoofed mammal also known as the mouse deer.

- *Archaeomeryx* had a three-chambered stomach, each of which broke down its plant food a little bit further.

- **Camels** were the next ruminants to evolve. One large prehistoric camel was *Aepycamelus*, which had a very long giraffe-like neck.

- **They were followed** by cattle, sheep and deer, which were more advanced ruminants because they had four-chambered stomachs.

- **The four chambers** of ruminants' stomachs are called the rumen, the reticulum, the omasum and the abosmasum.

- **Ruminants' big advantage** over other plant eaters was that they could decide when to digest their food. If they sensed a threat while they were eating they could run away and digest their meal later.

- **Camels and chevrotains** are the only surviving ruminants with three-chambered stomachs.

▲ Like other ruminants, these Arabian camels, or dromedaries, use urea, a bodily waste product, to feed the bacteria in their stomach chambers that break down plant matter. Less urea waste means less urine and so less water loss – which is why camels can cope with desert conditions.

Condylarths

- **Condylarths** were the first hoofed mammals.

- **They lived** in the Early Tertiary Period, between 65 and 40 mya.

- **All later hoofed mammals** from horses to pigs, are descended from condylarths.

- **The earliest condylarths** had claws as opposed to hooves.

- **Later ones** evolved longer limbs, tipped with nails or hooves, for running away quickly from carnivores.

- **The first known** condylarth was *Protungulatum*, a rabbit-sized plant eater.

- **A slightly later** condylarth was *Phenacodus*, which palaeontologists think was an insectivore (an insect eater).

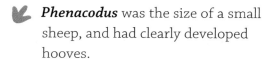 **Phenacodus** was the size of a small sheep, and had clearly developed hooves.

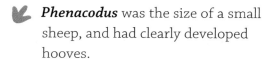 **Condylarths** spread over most of the world, including Europe, Asia, South America and Africa.

DID YOU KNOW?

Early condylarths were also rabbit-sized. Later ones, however, were as big as bears.

▲ *All hoofed mammals descend from condylarths, such as this* Hyopsodus. *The rat-sized, forest-dwelling* Hyopsodus, *however, had claws rather than hooves.*

313

Perissodactyls

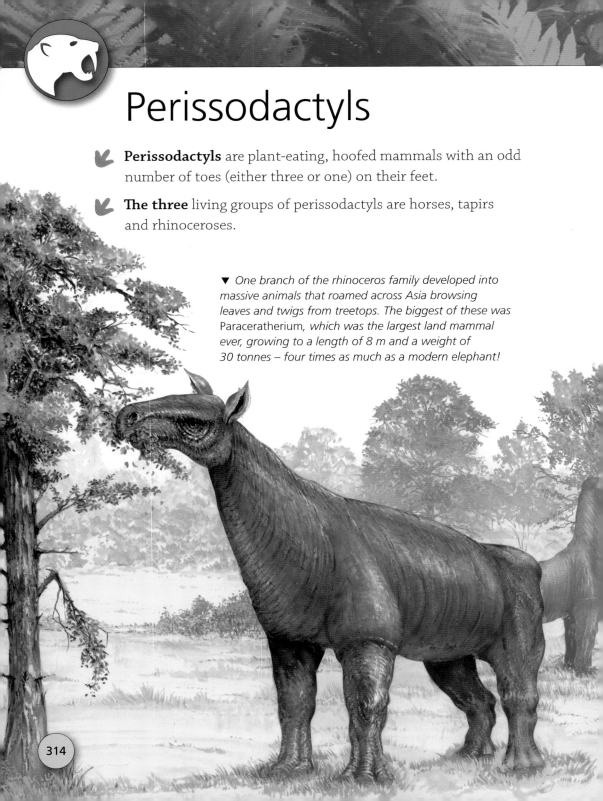

- **Perissodactyls** are plant-eating, hoofed mammals with an odd number of toes (either three or one) on their feet.

- **The three** living groups of perissodactyls are horses, tapirs and rhinoceroses.

▼ One branch of the rhinoceros family developed into massive animals that roamed across Asia browsing leaves and twigs from treetops. The biggest of these was Paraceratherium, which was the largest land mammal ever, growing to a length of 8 m and a weight of 30 tonnes – four times as much as a modern elephant!

- **The two** extinct groups of perissodactyls are brontotheres and chalicotheres.

- **Brontotheres** included massive beasts, such as *Brontotherium*, which had elephant-like limbs and a blunt, bony prong jutting from its nose. It ate only soft-leaved plants.

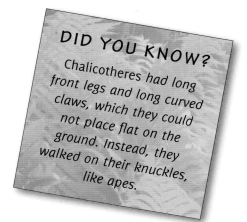

DID YOU KNOW?

Chalicotheres had long front legs and long curved claws, which they could not place flat on the ground. Instead, they walked on their knuckles, like apes.

- *Chalicotherium* was a chalicothere. It lacked front teeth, and ate by placing soft plant shoots in the back of its mouth, like a modern panda.

- **The earliest ancestors** of modern horses, tapirs and rhinos, appeared about 50 mya.

- *Miotapirus* was an ancestor of modern tapirs. It lived in North America about 20 mya.

- **Perissodactyls' feet** carried the weight of the animal on the middle toe, either in a single hoof, as in horses, or a big toe with one on each side, as in tapirs and rhinos.

- **For much of the Tertiary Period** (65–1.6 mya), perissodactyls were the most abundant form of hoofed mammals. They then declined, however, and artiodactyls (even-toed mammals) became dominant.

Artiodactyls

- **Artiodactyls** are hoofed mammals with an even number (either two or four) of toes on their feet.

- **Pigs**, camels, giraffe, sheep, goats, cattle, hippopotamuses, deer, antelopes and their ancestors are all artiodactyls.

- **Like the perissodactyls**, artiodactyls first appeared about 50 mya.

- *Dichobune* was an early artiodactyl, which lived between 40 and 30 mya. It had short limbs and four-toed feet.

- **In smaller artiodactyls**, such as sheep and goats, the foot is often divided into two parts (toes).

- **In very heavy artiodactyls**, such as hippopotamuses, there are four toes to carry the animal's weight.

- **At least two** of the middle toes on artiodactyls' feet carry an equal weight.

- **During the Miocene Epoch** (23–5 mya), artiodactyls became the most successful hoofed mammals.

- **Their success** lay more in their stomachs than in their feet. Artiodactyls evolved more advanced digestive systems, which allowed them to process the tough grasses that had replaced the earlier, softer, forest plants.

- **Another difference** between artiodactyls and perissodactyls is their ankle bones. Artiodactyls' ankle bones have more rounded joints at both ends, which means they provide more thrust when they run.

▲ This cow and her calf are members of the most successful group of hoofed mammals to have evolved – the artiodactyls. There are around 150 living species of artiodactyl.

Enteloodonts

Enteloodonts were large piglike mammals that lived in Asia and North America in the Miocene Epoch (23–5 mya).

▼ *The fierce-looking* Dinohyus, *also known as* Daeodon, *may well have scavenged for its food like modern hyenas. Its powerful neck muscles and large canine teeth suggest it could have broken bones and eaten flesh.*

- **These mammals are** the ancestors of modern pigs.

- **One of the largest** entelodonts was *Dinohyus*. It stood at least 2 m tall at the shoulder with a skull that was around one metre long.

- *Dinohyus* probably fed off plant roots or scavenged for prey.

- *Dinohyus* had very distinctive teeth. Its incisors (front teeth) were blunt, but the teeth next to them, the canines, were sturdy and substantial, and could have been used for defence.

- **Another entelodont** was the scavenger *Entelodon*, the largest of which was about the same size as *Dinohyus*.

- **There are severe wounds** in the fossils of some *Entelodon* skulls, such as a 2-cm-deep gash in the bone between its eyes. Palaeontologists think these were caused by the animals fighting amongst themselves.

- *Entelodon* **means** 'perfect-toothed', and this mammal had a thick layer of enamel on its teeth.

- **However, many fossil** remains of *Entelodon* have broken teeth – a result of the tough, varied diet of this scavenger.

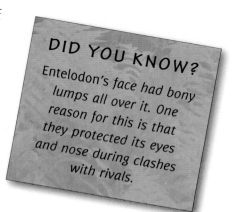

DID YOU KNOW?

Entelodon's face had bony lumps all over it. One reason for this is that they protected its eyes and nose during clashes with rivals.

Bats

- *Icaronycteris* is the earliest known bat. Its fossil remains are between 55 and 45 million years old.

- **Despite its age**, *Icaronycteris* looks very similar to a modern bat. It has a bat's typically large ears, which it probably used as a sonar, like modern bats.

- **One difference** from modern bats was that *Icaronycteris'* tail was not joined to its legs by flaps of skin.

- **Palaeontologists** think that there must have been earlier, more primitive-looking bats from which *Icaronycteris* evolved.

DID YOU KNOW?
Bats are the only mammals that are known to have reached Australia after it became isolated from the rest of the world around 40 mya.

The chance of finding earlier prehistoric bat fossils is very small – like birds, bats have very fragile skeletons that do not fossilize well.

- *Icaronycteris* **ate insects**. Palaeontologists know this because they have found insect remains in the part of the fossil where its stomach would have been.

▶ The earliest bats belong to the group known as Microchiroptera, the smaller insect-eating bats that are the most numerous today. These bats are characterized by having the large ears and noses needed for echo-location of insect prey.

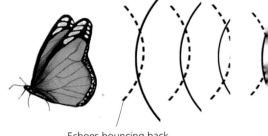

Echoes bouncing back
off the butterfly

- *Icaronycteris* fossils have been found in North America.
- **The fossil remains** of another prehistoric bat, *Palaeochiropteryx*, have been found in Europe.
- **Like *Icaronycteris***, this bat seems to have been an insectivore (insect eater).

Sound waves from the bat

Elephant evolution

Elephants and their ancestors belong to an order of animals called Proboscidea, meaning 'long-snouted'. Another word for elephants is proboscideans.

The ancestors of elephants appeared around 40 mya. They were trunkless and looked a bit like large pigs.

▼ Phiomia *had a well-formed trunk as well as two pairs of tusks – a pair on its upper jaw, projecting out and then down, and a pair on its lower jaw.*

- **Moeritherium** is the earliest known of these elephant ancestors. Its name comes from Lake Moeris in Egypt, where fossil-hunters first discovered its remains.

- **The American palaeontologist** Henry Fairfield Osborn (1857–1935) described *Moeritherium* as 'a missing link' between elephants and other mammals.

- **Moeritherium was 3 m long**, weighed 200 kg, and probably spent much of its life wallowing in rivers or shallow lakes, like a hippopotamus.

- **The next step** in the development of elephants was taken by *Phiomia*, which lived about 36 mya.

  - **Phiomia** is the first known of a group of elephants called mastodonts. Its shoulder height could be up to 2.4 m, and it lived in swampy areas.

    - **One group** of elephants that descended from *Phiomia* were the deinotheres, which had one pair of enormous downward curving tusks in the lower jaw.

    - **The other groups** that evolved from the mastodonts were the true elephants (which resemble living elephants) and the mammoths. These animals appeared in the Pliocene Epoch (5–1.6 mya).

323

Woolly mammoth

- **Woolly mammoths** (scientific name *Mammuthus primigenius*) lived between 120,000 and 6000 years ago.

- **They lived** on the steppes of Russia and Asia and the plains of North America during the ice ages of the Quaternary Period (1.6 mya to the present).

- **To survive** these cold places, woolly mammoths were designed for warmth and insulation.

- **Their woolly coats** were made up of two layers of hair – an outside layer of long, coarse hairs, and a second layer of densely packed bristles.

- **Woolly mammoths also had** very tough skins – up to 2.5 cm thick – beneath which was a deep layer of fat.

- **Male woolly mammoths** could grow up to 3.5 m long and 2.9 m high at the shoulder, and weigh up to 2.75 tonnes.

- **They had** long tusks that curved forward, up and then back. They used their tusks to defend themselves against attackers and probably to clear snow and ice to reach low-lying plants.

DID YOU KNOW?
People often think the woolly mammoth had red hair, but in fact this colour was a chemical reaction that happened after the animal died.

● **Some cave paintings** by Cro-Magnon humans clearly depict woolly mammoths.

● **Many excellently preserved** woolly mammoth remains have been discovered in the permanently frozen ground of Siberia.

▼ *Woolly mammoths had thick, shaggy fur to keep them warm, small ears and enormous tusks.*

Rhinoceroses

- **Rhinoceroses** were a very important group of mammals in the Tertiary Period (65–1.6 mya).

- *Hyracodon* was an early rhino that lived in North America about 30 mya.

- **Long, slender legs** meant that *Hyracodon* would have been a fast runner. It grew to about 1.5 m long.

- **Amynodonts** were a group of prehistoric rhinos that experts believed evolved from *Hyracodon*.

- *Metamynodon* was an amynodont rhino. It was as large as a hippopotamus and may have had a similar lifestyle to one, wading in rivers and lakes.

- **True rhinoceroses**, the ancestors of modern rhinos, were another group that descended from early rhinos such as *Hyracodon*.

- **One of the first** true rhinos was *Trigonias*, which had four toes on its front feet but three on its hind feet. It lived in the Oligocene Epoch (37–24 mya).

- *Caenopus*, another true rhino, had three toes on all four feet. This was the pattern for all later rhinos.

- **The largest rhinoceros** horn of all time belonged to *Elasmotherium*, which lived in Europe about 500,000 years ago. The horn was a massive 2 m long.

- **Rhinos became extinct** in North America between 5 and 1.6 mya, and later in Europe. But they survived in Asia and Africa and continue to do so today, although they too are threatened by extinction.

◀ *Hunted for their horns, which some people value as medicine, all the world's rhinoceroses are endangered.*

Brontotherium

Brontotherium was a large herbivore, whose name means 'thunder beast'.

It lived in North America and central Asia around 40 mya.

Brontotherium was somewhere between a rhinoceros and an elephant in size. It was 2.5 m tall at its shoulders.

It belonged to the group of mammals called perissodactyls – hoofed mammals with an odd number of toes.

Brontotherium **had thick legs** and short, broad feet with four toes on its front feet and three toes on its hind feet.

- **On the top of its snout**, *Brontotherium* had a thick, Y-shaped horn.

- **Palaeontologists** think that *Brontotherium* used its horn to ward off predators and to fight rival males.

- ***Brontotherium*** lived in herds on grassy plains and in forests.

- **It had big,** square molar teeth that crushed the soft leaves it fed on.

> **DID YOU KNOW?**
> Brontotherium is a distant cousin of modern horses, tapirs and rhinoceroses.

◀ *Male* Brontotherium*s had larger two-pronged horns than females, which suggests that males used them for display and for fighting.*

329

First horses

Horses have one of the best fossil records of any animal. Palaeontologists have been able to trace their evolution from the earliest horselike mammals to the modern horse.

Hyracotherium is the first known horse. It lived in forests in North America and Europe in the Late Palaeocene and Early Eocene Epochs (60–50 mya).

▼ Hyracotherium *is the earliest known horse. Over time, horses became the best adapted of all hoofed animals for life on the open plains.*

- **Another name** for *Hyracotherium* is *Eohippus*, which means 'dawn horse'.

- *Hyracotherium* was the size of a fox. It had a short neck, a long tail and slender limbs. It also had three toes on its hind feet and four toes on its front feet.

- *Mesohippus* was one of the horses to evolve next after *Hyracotherium*, between 40 and 25 mya. Its name means 'middle horse'.

- *Mesohippus* had longer legs than *Hyracotherium* and would have been a faster runner.

- **It would also** have been better at chewing food, because its teeth had a larger surface area.

- **An improved** chewing ability was important for horses and other plant eaters as forests gave way to grasslands, and more abundant but tougher plants.

- *Mesohippus* had also evolved three toes on its front feet to match the three on its hind feet.

- **As horses** evolved, they migrated from North America and Europe to Asia, Africa and South America.

Later horses

🐾 **Merychippus**, which lived between 11 and 5 mya, represented a leap forward from earlier horses, such as *Mesohippus*. It was the size of a pony.

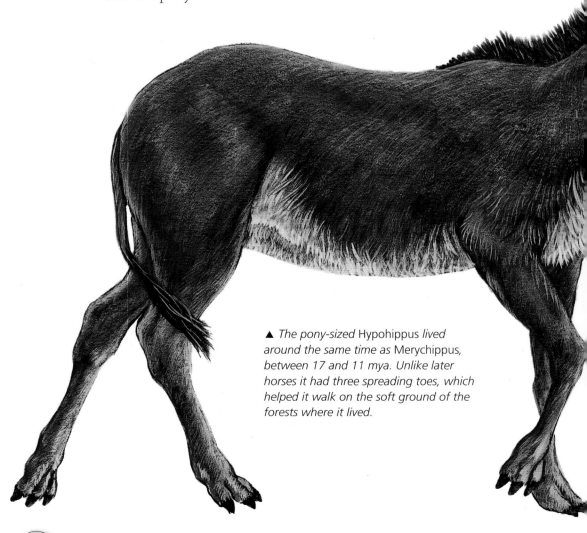

▲ *The pony-sized* Hypohippus *lived around the same time as* Merychippus, *between 17 and 11 mya. Unlike later horses it had three spreading toes, which helped it walk on the soft ground of the forests where it lived.*

 **It was the first horse** to eat only grass, and – to help it reach the grass – had a longer neck and muzzle (snout) than earlier horses.

 *Merychippus'* middle toe had also evolved into a hoof, although this hoof did not have a pad on the bottom, unlike modern horses.

 **The legs** of *Merychippus* were designed for outrunning carnivores. Its upper leg bones were shorter than previous horses, the lower leg bones were longer.

 **Shorter upper leg bones** meant that the horse's main leg-moving muscles could be packed in at the top of the leg – which translates into a faster-running animal.

 *Hipparion*, which means 'better horse', was a further advance on *Merychippus*. It had thinner legs and more horselike hooves. *Hipparion* lived between 15 and 2 mya.

 **An even more advanced** horse was *Pliohippus*. The side toes that *Hipparion* still had vanished, making *Pliohippus* the first one-toed horse.

 *Pliohippus'* **teeth** were similar to those of modern horses – they were long and had an uneven surface for grinding up grass.

 *Equus*, the modern horse and the latest stage in the evolution of the animal, first appeared around 2 mya.

First whales

The very first whales looked nothing like the enormous creatures that swim in our oceans today.

Ambulocetus, one of the first members of the whale family, looked more like a giant otter. It lived about 50 mya.

Ambulocetus means 'walking whale', and it spent more time on land than in water.

▶ Pakicetus *could run fast and swim well. It probably lived alongside rivers and streams and hunted animals both in and out of the water.*

It would, however, have been a good swimmer. Fossil remains show that *Ambulocetus* had webbed feet and hands.

An even earlier whale ancestor than *Ambulocetus* was *Pakicetus*, which lived about 52 mya.

> *Pakicetus* **is named** after the country Pakistan, where a fossil of its skull was found in 1979.

> *Pakicetus* was around 1.8 m long. *Ambulocetus*, at 3 m, was bigger.

> **Palaeontologists** think that whales evolved from carnivorous hoofed mammals called mesonychids.

Around 40 mya, the first true whales, which swam only, evolved from their half-walking, half-swimming ancestors.

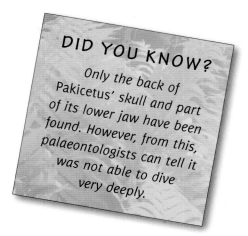

DID YOU KNOW?

Only the back of *Pakicetus*' skull and part of its lower jaw have been found. However, from this, palaeontologists can tell it was not able to dive very deeply.

Later whales

- **First appearing** about 40 mya, *Basilosaurus* closely resembled whales we are familiar with today, more so than its ancestors *Pakicetus* and *Ambulocetus*.

- **It was also enormous!** It measured between 20 and 25 m long – the same as three elephants standing in a row.

- ***Basilosaurus* had** a variety of teeth in its mouth – sharp teeth at the front for stabbing, and saw-edged teeth at the back for chewing.

- **These whales ate** large fish, squid, and other marine mammals.

DID YOU KNOW?

Cetotherium was a prehistoric baleen whale that first appeared 15 mya. Instead of teeth, these whales had hard plates in their mouths, called baleen, that filtered plankton and small fish.

🐾 **There were some** big differences between *Basilosaurus* and modern whales. For a start, it had a slimmer body.

🐾 *Basilosaurus* **also lacked** a blowhole, a nostril on the top of modern whales' heads that they breathe out of when they come to the surface. Instead, *Basilosaurus* had nostrils on its snout.

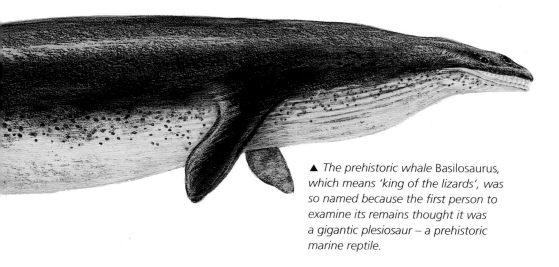

▲ *The prehistoric whale* Basilosaurus, *which means 'king of the lizards', was so named because the first person to examine its remains thought it was a gigantic plesiosaur – a prehistoric marine reptile.*

🐾 **A more advanced whale** than *Basilosaurus* was *Prosqualodon*. It lived between 30 and 20 mya and had a blowhole.

🐾 *Prosqualodon* **may have been** the ancestor of toothed whales, a group that includes sperm whales, killer whales, beaked whales and dolphins.

🐾 *Prosqualodon* looked similar to a dolphin. It had a long, streamlined body and a long, narrow snout, which was full of pointed teeth.

337

Humans

Early primates

- **The primates** are a group of mammals that include lemurs, monkeys, apes and humans.

- **Primates** have a much greater range of movement in their arms, legs, fingers and toes than other mammals.

- **They also have** a more acute sense of touch because their fingers and toes end in flat nails, not curved claws – so the skin underneath evolved into a sensitive pad.

- **The ancestors** of primates were small insectivorous (insect eating) mammals that looked like shrews.

- **The first known primate** was *Plesiadapis*, which lived about 60 mya in Europe and North America. It was a squirrel-like tree climber.

- **More advanced primates** developed about 10 million years later. They looked a bit like modern lemurs.

- *Notharctus* was one of these lemur-like primates. It ate leaves and fruit, was about 40 cm long, and had a grasping thumb that would have gripped well to branches.

- **Other more advanced** – but still early – primates include *Smilodectes* and *Tetonius*. They had larger brains and eyes, longer tails and smaller snouts than *Plesiadapis*.

- **These animals** were the ancestors of tarsiers, lemurs and lorises, but not the higher primates – the monkeys, apes and humans. Palaeontologists believe that role belongs to the omomyid primates.

One early monkey was *Mesopithecus*, which lived eight mya in Greece and Turkey. It was similar to modern monkeys in many ways, but had a longer tail.

▼ *The early primate* Plesiadapis *had a long tail and claws on its fingers and toes – unlike later monkeys and apes, which had nails.*

Apes

Apes are primates that have more complex brains than monkeys and no tails. Hominids (early humans) evolved from apes.

Aegyptopithecus was one of the ancestors of apes. It lived in Egypt in the Oligocene Epoch (37–24 mya). It was small and had a short tail.

An early ape that lived between 23 and 14 mya was *Proconsul*. Its body size varied from that of a small monkey to that of a female gorilla, and it had a larger brain than *Aegyptopithecus*.

▼ The early ape Dryopithecus *stood about one metre tall. It had the largest brain for its size of any mammal and flourished in open grassland regions in Africa, Asia and Europe.*

- *Proconsul* **was a fruit eater**. Palaeontologists think that it walked on four limbs with part of its weight supported by the knuckles of its hands, like modern chimpanzees and gorillas.

- **Two lines of apes** developed after *Proconsul*. From one line came gibbons and orang-utans, from the other chimpanzees, gorillas and humans.

- *Dryopithecus* was a chimplike ape that evolved after *Proconsul* and lived in the Miocene Epoch (23–5 mya). It may have stood on two legs but climbed using all four.

- *Ramapithecus* was an ape that lived in the Middle and Late Miocene Epoch. It is now thought to be part of the chain of evolution of Asian apes and is possibly an ancestor of the orang-utan.

- **Australopithecines** were a further step in the evolution from apes to humans. Australopithecines (meaning 'southern apes') walked on two legs.

- **The biggest-ever ape** was *Gigantopithecus*, which lived in China until around one mya. It may have been up to 2.5 m tall and weighed 300 kg.

Early hominids

- **One of the earliest known** hominids (early humans) is *Ardipithecus ramidus*, which lived about 4.5 mya.

- **It would have looked** similar to a chimpanzee in many ways, except for one major difference – *Ardipithecus ramidus* walked on two legs.

- **It lived** in woods and forests, sleeping in trees at night, but foraging on the ground for roots during the day.

- **A full-grown** *Ardipithecus ramidus* male was about 1.3 m tall and weighed about 27 kg.

- **Archaeologists** discovered the teeth, skull and arm bone fossils of *Ardipithecus ramidus* in Ethiopia in 1994.

- **In 2001**, archaeologists in Ethiopia found the remains of an even older hominid, *Ardipithecus ramidus kadabba*, which lived between 5.6 and 5.8 mya.

- **The fossils** of *Ardipithecus ramidus kadabba* are similar to those of *Ardipithecus ramidus*, so it is possible both are very closely related.

- **Some scientists argue**, however, that *Ardipithecus ramidus kadabba* is closer to an ape than a hominid.

- ***Australopithecus anamensis*** is a later hominid than *Ardipithecus ramidus*. Its fossils date to between 4.2 and 3.9 million years old.

- **A fossil** of one of *Australopithecus anamensis'* knee-joints shows that it shifted its weight from one leg to the other when it moved – a sure sign that it walked on two legs.

▲ Ardipithecus ramidus. *Scientists chose its name from the Afar language of Ethiopia – 'ardi' means 'ground' while 'ramid' means 'root' – words that express its position at the base of human history.*

Australopithecus africanus

- *Australopithecus africanus*, which means 'the southern ape of Africa', was an early hominid that emerged between 2.8 and 2.3 mya.

- *Australopithecus africanus* was the first australopithecine to be discovered.

- **The Australian-born** scientist Raymond Dart made the discovery of this important fossil in South Africa in 1924.

- **The fossil** Dart identified was found in a quarry near the village of Taung, on the edge of the Kalahari Desert.

- **It was the fossil** of a skull, belonging to a child around two or three years old. The fossil became known as the Taung child.

- **Many people** didn't believe in Dart's discovery – they thought the find was an ape, not a hominid. But one person did believe it – the archaeologist Robert Broom.

- **In 1947**, Broom himself found a skull of an adult *Australopithecus africanus*.

- **The adult skull** became known as 'Mrs Ples' because Broom first thought it belonged to a different species, *Plesianthropus transvaalensis*.

- **By the 1950s** other parts of *Australopithecus africanus*' skeleton had been unearthed, including a pelvis and a femur.

- **These fossils proved** beyond doubt that *Australopithecus africanus* was an upright-walking hominid.

▼ *The Taung child may have looked like this. Marks on the skull, and remains of a large eggshell nearby, suggest a big bird killed the child.*

Homo habilis

Homo habilis is one of the earliest known members of the genus *Homo*, to which we also belong. It lived between 2.4 and 1.6 mya.

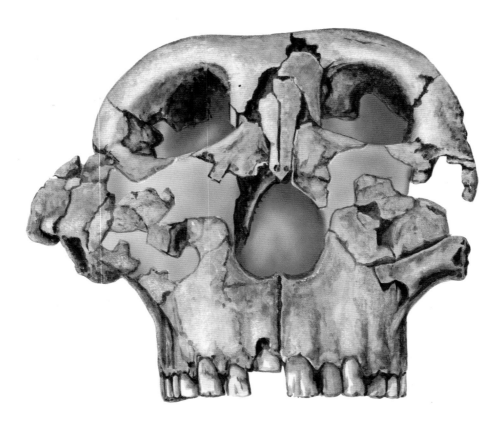

▲ *The first* Homo habilis *skull found by Louis and Mary Leakey in Tanzania.* Homo habilis *had a bigger brain than any previous hominid.*

- **The archaeologists** Louis and Mary Leakey first discovered its remains at Olduvai Gorge in Tanzania, in 1961.

- **Fossils** of *Homo habilis* skulls have since been found around Lake Turkana in Kenya, one of the richest sites for hominid fossils in the world.

DID YOU KNOW?
Homo habilis used stone tools to crack open animal bones so it could eat the nutritious marrow inside.

- **The skulls** show that *Homo habilis* had a flat face with prominent cheekbones, similar to australopithecines, which it would have lived alongside.

- *Homo habilis* was much more apelike than its successor, *Homo ergaster*. It had fur and lacked any form of language.

- **But it did have** a bigger brain than any australopithecine. It also had more flexible hands and straighter, more sensitive fingers.

- *Homo habilis* means 'handy man' – it could use its hands to gather fruit and crack nuts. It also created the first stone tools.

- **A fully grown** *Homo habilis* male was around 1.5 m tall and weighed about 50 kg.

Homo erectus

- **About 1.6 million years ago** a new form of human appeared in Africa – *Homo erectus*. Some scientists think that a similar form, *Homo ergaster*, may have been a type of *Homo erectus*.

- **The body of** *Homo erectus* was almost identical to that of a modern human, though it seems to have been about 10 cm shorter on average.

- **The head was rather different** to that of modern humans, having a heavy ridge of bone over the eyes and protruding jaws that made it look more apelike.

- **Some remains indicate** that *Homo erectus* was capable of building huts out of wood and brushwood. These were probably temporary shelters for a tribe on the move, not permanent homes.

- ***Homo erectus*** spread beyond Africa and settled in Europe and Asia.

- **In the late 19th century**, Eugène Dubois discovered *Homo erectus* fossils on the Indonesian island of Java. He was a famous Dutch palaeoanthropologist (someone who studies hominid fossils).

- **In the 1930s**, archaeologists discovered more than 40 *Homo erectus* skeletons in China.

DID YOU KNOW?
The 'Peking Man' fossils disappeared at the beginning of the World War II and have never been found. They were confiscated by Japanese troops just when they were about to be shipped to the USA.

The archaeologists also found evidence that *Homo erectus* used fire and practised cannibalism.

For a long time, people called the human to which the Chinese fossils belonged 'Peking Man'. It was much later that palaeoanthropologists realized it was, in fact, *Homo erectus*.

▼ *Stone hearths that were used by* Homo erectus *prove that it had mastered fire. Fire provided warmth, light, protection and the means to cook food.*

351

Homo neanderthalensis

- *Homo neanderthalensis* – or Neanderthals – lived between 230,000 and 28,000 years ago across Europe, Russia and parts of the Middle East.

- *Homo neanderthalensis* **means** 'man from the Neander Valley', which is the site in Germany where the first of its fossil remains were found in 1865.

- **Neanderthals** are our extinct cousins rather than our direct ancestors – they are from a different branch of the human family.

- **They were** about 30 percent heavier than modern humans. Their bodies were more sturdy and they had shorter legs.

- **Neanderthals'** shorter, stockier bodies were better suited than modern humans to life in Europe and Russia during the ice ages of the Pleistocene Epoch (1.6 million to 10,000 years ago).

- **Their faces** were also different, with sloping foreheads and heavy brow ridges.

- **They buried** their dead, cooked meat and made various tools and weapons.

- **Neanderthals** made the first ever spears tipped with stone blades.

DID YOU KNOW?

Many people think that Neanderthals were slow and stupid, but in fact their brains were at least as big as modern human's.

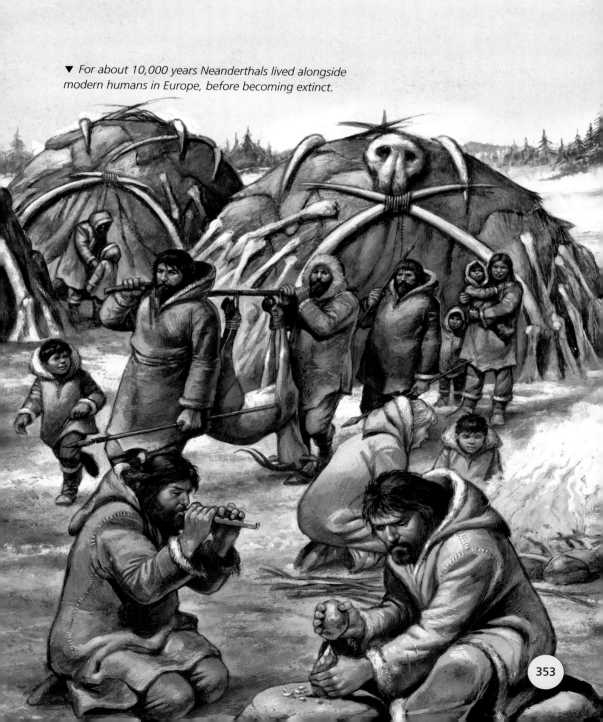

▼ *For about 10,000 years Neanderthals lived alongside modern humans in Europe, before becoming extinct.*

Homo sapiens

- *Homo sapiens* – meaning 'wise man' – first appeared in Africa around 150,000 years ago. This is the species to which human beings belong.

- **The first** *Homo sapiens* outside Africa appeared in Israel 90,000 years ago.

- **By 40,000 years ago,** *Homo sapiens* had spread to many parts of the world, including Europe and Borneo.

- **We call the humans** that settled in Europe Cro-Magnons. They dressed in furs and hunted with spears and nets.

- **Cro-Magnons** had a basic language and culture, which included painting images on cave walls.

- **Similar to modern humans**, Cro-Magnons had marginally bigger jaws and noses and more rounded braincases (the part of the skull that encloses the brain).

▶ *Cave painting, cooking and complicated tool-making are all features of early* Homo sapiens. Homo sapiens *also look different from other human species, having a higher forehead and a more prominent chin.*

Homo sapiens probably arrived in North America about 30,000 years ago.

These people would have crossed the Bering land bridge – formed by shrunken sea levels during the then ice age – from present-day Siberia to present-day Alaska.

The earliest known human culture in North America is that of the Clovis people, which is thought to be around 11,500 years old.

355

Brains and intelligence

- **Primates**, from which hominids descended, had bigger brains in relation to their body size than other mammals.

- **Primates developed** larger brains – and more intelligence – because living in and moving between trees required a high degree of balance, coordination and the skilful use of hands and feet.

- **Once hominids' brains** started getting bigger, so their skulls began to change. Bigger brains led to the development of foreheads.

- *Homo habilis'* **brain** was 50 percent bigger than its australopithecine predecessors. It had a brain capacity of 750 ml.

- **The structure** of its brain was different to that of earlier hominids. It had much bigger frontal lobes – the parts of the brain associated with planning and problem-solving.

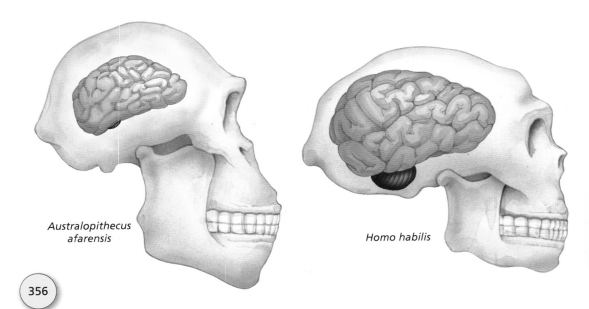

Australopithecus afarensis

Homo habilis

- **Homo habilis** put its greater intelligence to use in the quest to find meat, which it scavenged from other animals' kills to supplement its diet.

- **Eating more meat** allowed hominids' brains to get even bigger. Breaking down plant food uses up a huge amount of energy, so the fewer plants hominids ate, the more energy was available for their brains.

- **Homo ergaster** had an even bigger brain, with a capacity of around 1000 ml. It could use this intelligence to read tracks left by animals – a major development in hunting.

- **The brain** of *Homo erectus* became larger during its existence. About one mya its brain capacity was 1000 ml, 500,000 years later it was 1300 ml.

- **Our brain capacity** is 1750 ml.

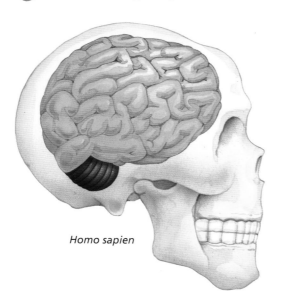

Homo sapien

◄ *Brain size is linked to intelligence, but size isn't everything! What makes humans and our ancestors intelligent is our brain's complex structure.*

Language

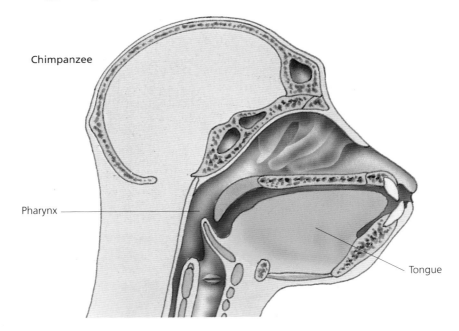

- **Language** may go back as far as *Homo erectus* or even *Homo ergaster* – although this would have been a very, very simple form of communication.

- **Language developed** as a way of maintaining relationships within groups.

- **Language is different** from cries of alarm or mating calls. It involves a system for representing ideas and feelings.

- **Speech requires** a long pharynx – a tube in the neck that runs up from the vocal cords (contained in the larynx) to the mouth.

- **In other primates** the pharynx is too short to produce complex modifications of sound.

- *Homo ergaster* had a longer pharynx than earlier hominids, suggesting that it was able to produce some basic speech.

Chimpanzee

Pharynx

Tongue

- **Homo heidelbergensis** had an even longer pharynx and would have been able to produce complex sounds. However, its speech would have differed from ours because of the different shape of its face.

- **Neanderthals** would also have been able to speak. The fossil remains of a Neanderthal hyoid bone, which supports the larynx, is almost identical to a modern human's.

- **Modern speech** only developed with the arrival of *Homo sapiens*.

- **Some experts** think that modern speech first took place 100,000 years ago – others think it did not happen until around 40,000 years ago.

Human

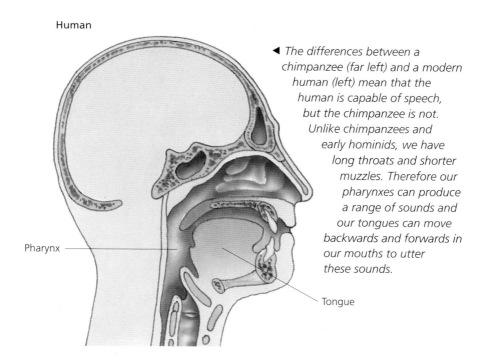

◀ The differences between a chimpanzee (far left) and a modern human (left) mean that the human is capable of speech, but the chimpanzee is not. Unlike chimpanzees and early hominids, we have long throats and shorter muzzles. Therefore our pharynxes can produce a range of sounds and our tongues can move backwards and forwards in our mouths to utter these sounds.

Pharynx

Tongue

359

Tools

▲ Homo habilis *produced flakes of stone, such as this one, by striking one stone against another, called a hammerstone.*

🐾 **The greatest number** of *Homo habilis* tools has been found in the Olduvai Gorge in Tanzania. They include rocks that were used as hammers, flakers, choppers and scrapers.

🐾 *Homo habilis* used these tools to cut meat and, especially, to scrape open animal bones to eat the marrow inside.

🐾 **The stone tools** used by *Homo habilis* are crude and basic. This hominid was the first tool-maker, but, hardly surprisingly, it was not a skilled one.

🐾 **Making these** early stone tools was still a challenging task – the tool-maker needed to strike one rock with another so that it would produce a single, sharp flake rather than shattering into many pieces.

▼ Homo ergaster *used hammers made of bone to produce thinner and sharper flakes of stone.*

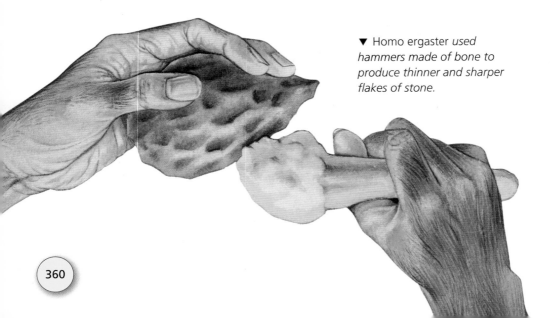

- **Tool-making requires** considerable intelligence. It involves the use of memory, as well as the ability to plan ahead and to solve abstract problems.

- ***Homo ergaster's*** tools were much more advanced. This hominid made tear-drop shaped, symmetrical hand axes called 'Acheulean axes', after the place in France where similar axes have been discovered from a later period.

- **Neanderthals** developed a method for producing razor-sharp flakes of stone, called Levallois flakes, which could be placed on the end of spears.

- **This method** required great precision and dexterity. While modern humans have a much broader range of skills, they would be very hard pushed to produce such tools themselves.

- **Modern humans** developed the greatest variety of tools. Cro-Magnon tools include knives, spearpoints and engraving tools.

- **Cro-Magnon humans** also began to make tools from materials other than stone, including wood, bones, antlers and ivory.

▲ Homo sapiens' *tools became more and more complex. They incorporated different materials, such as twine in the axe (top) and, in this saw (bottom), flint teeth held in place by resin.*

Hunting

- **One of the earliest** human hunters was *Homo erectus*. Other hominids that came before it, like *Homo habilis*, may have hunted small or lame animals, but they mostly scavenged other animals' kills.

- *Homo erectus* used fire to drive animals into traps. They also developed handaxes, which they used to kill animals or butcher them once they were dead.

- **It was the Neanderthals** that excelled in hunting – a skill they developed during the ice ages of the Pleistocene Epoch (1.6–0.01 mya).

- **Hunting developed** into a way of providing not only food, but also clothing (animal skins) and materials for tools (bones, horns and hooves).

- **Neanderthals used nets** or spears to catch spawning fish. They also hunted seals by spearing them through holes in the ice or by throwing spears at them.

- **In the 1990s**, finds of Neanderthal weapons in Boxgrove, England, showed the full range of this species' hunting arsenal. They include axes, slicing knives, cutting blades and slashing blades.

- **As well as hunting** for meat, hominids also gathered wild fruits, vegetables and nuts.

- **Another Neanderthal site** at Schöningen in Germany, preserved the remains of nine polished wooden spears, made from a spruce tree.

Each of these spears was over 2 m long, and was designed to be thrown like a javelin.

Homo sapiens developed new weapons for hunting, including the bow and arrow, the blowpipe and the boomerang.

▼ *Early humans developed more and more sophisticated methods of killing animals, including weapons, traps and fire.*

Cave paintings

- **Cro-Magnon** people produced many cave paintings.

- **One of the best** examples is the Grotte de Chauvet in the Ardeche, France, which was discovered in 1994.

- **The Grotte de Chauvet** caves contain more than 300 drawings of animals, from lions and deer to buffalos and woolly rhinoceroses.

- **People used to be** very sceptical that early humans could have produced cave paintings and thought they were hoaxes.

- **Another magnificent example** of cave painting is that of the Altamira cave in northern Spain, which has an 18-m-long ceiling covered with red-, black- and violet-coloured paintings of bison.

- **Most cave paintings** date from around 20,000 to 15,000 years ago, when Cro-Magnon man lived in Europe and elsewhere.

- **Other cave paintings** may be much older. Some archaeologists think that the Grotte de Chauvet paintings are 33,000 years old.

- **No one can say** for sure what cave art means. Many appear to represent hunting scenes, but there are also many symbols in caves, including patterns of squares and dots.

- **Another very common image** in caves is that of a human hand.

> **DID YOU KNOW?**
> Cro-Magnon people made hand outlines by blowing a sooty pigment over their hand as they pressed it against the cave wall.

▲ *A series of cave paintings known as the Great Hall of Bulls in Lascaux, south-west France. The paintings are around 15,000 years old.*

Index

Index

Entries in **bold** refer to main subject entries; entries in *italics* refer to illustrations.

heads 22, 33, 35, 38, *39*,
    43, 47, 51, 60, *60*, 68,
    69, 74, 77, 91, 92, 96,
    97, 103, 114, 118,
    121, 122, 128, 131,
    133, 134, 138, 149,
    152, *152*, *154*, 162,
    166, *168*, 170, *170*,
    171, *171*, 179, *179*,
    180, 189, *264*, 265,
    272, 278, *278*, 282,
    307, 337, 350
  foreheads *163*, 166,
    352, *354*, 356
Hemicyclaspis 34, 35
Hendrickson, Susan 273
Hennig, Edwin 254
Henodus 65
herbivores 56, **116–117**,
    205, *212*, 280, 294,
    298, 300, **306–307**,
    328
herds 85, 96, 157, 209,
    216–217, *216*, *218*,
    219
Herrerasaurus 82, *82*,
    83, 244, *244*, 257,
    257
Hesperocyon 304, *305*
Heterodontosaurus 103,
    158–159, *158*, *159*,
    197, 201
hibernation **220–221**
Hipparion 333
hips **196–197**, 206, 210,
    250, 251
  hip girdles 42
Homalocephale 171

hominids 342, **344–345**,
    346, *348*, 349, 356,
    358, *359*, 360, 361,
    362
Homo erectus **350–351**,
    351, 357, 358, 362
Homo ergaster 349, 350,
    357, 358, *360*, 361
Homo habilis **348–349**,
    348, 356, *356*, 357,
    360, *360*, 362
Homo heidelbergensis 359
Homo neanderthalensis
    352–353
Homo sapiens **354–355**,
    354, 357, 359, 361,
    363
hooves 215, 269, *292*,
    300, 312, 313, *313*,
    314, 315, 316, *317*,
    330, 333, 362, 363
horns 166, *167*, 168, 172,
    178–179, *179*, 184,
    184, 185, 202, 226,
    247, 272, 287, 309,
    327, 329, *329*, 362
horses 278, 296, 312, 314,
    329, **330–331**, *330*,
    332–333, *332*
horsetails 18, 116, 149, *231*
humans *279*, 297, 302,
    325, **338–365**, *353*,
    359, *363*
hunters 38, *38*, *75*, 83, 92,
    96, 104, 106, *190*,
    217, *278*, 279, 284,
    291, 297, 298, *301*,
    302, 304, *305*, *327*,

hunters (*cont.*)
    335, 354, 357,
    362–363, 364
Hyaenodon 298, 299
Hybodus 39
Hylaeosaurus 252
Hylonomus 50, 51
Hyopsodus 313,
Hypohippus 332,
Hypselosaurus 231
Hypsilophodon 231
Hyracodon 326
Hyracotherium 330, 331

I

Icaronycteris 320
ice ages 13, *303*, 324,
    352, 355, 362
ichthyosaurs 54, **70–71**,
    72, 265
Ichthyosaurus 70, *71*
Ichthyostega 44
Ichthyornis 282
Iguanodon **160–161**, *161*,
    173, 182, 184, *195*,
    201, 210, 215, 217,
    219, 230, 240, *240*,
    252
India 71, 234, *234*, 235
Indricotherium 268, 269
insectivores 290, 312, 321,
    340
insects 12, *13*, 24, 51, 54,
    74, 80, 83, 85, 102,
    202, 213, 246, 260,
    262, 280, 290, 293,
    320, *320*

P